The Clinical Christ

Scientific and Spiritual Reflections on the Transformative Psychology Called Christian Holism

The Clinical Christ

*Scientific and Spiritual Reflections
on the Transformative Psychology
Called Christian Holism*

Charles L. Zeiders, Psy.D.

Published by:
Julian's House
Birdsboro, PA

About the Author

Charles Zeiders is a Doctor of Psychology and a licensed psychologist. A Postdoctoral Fellow of the University of Pennsylvania's Center for Cognitive Therapy and a Diplomate in Cognitive-Behavioral Therapy (NACBT), Dr. Zeiders has lectured nationally and internationally regarding the interplay of spirituality and health. Throughout his career, Dr. Zeiders has produced academic publications on the psychology of religion, taught psychology at the University level, and worked with patients in the midst of Christian spiritual transformation. In independent practice in the Philadelphia area, Dr. Zeiders chairs the *Think Tank for Christian Holism.*

About the Cover Art

The cover design depicts the Icon of *Christian Holism.* Atop the cross, the dove represents the Holy Spirit's presence in the clinical situation, guiding and nurturing the clinical process so that therapy unfolds toward the patient's healing in a state of grace. The cross beam depicts God creating Adam, alluding to the fact that, though fallen, human nature contains the image of God, and that the final aim of *Christian Holism* involves participating in the Spirit's restoration of the Divine Image to every person who enters treatment. At the bottom of the cross, Freud represents the corpus of psychotherapeutic theory and practice—a body of knowledge that comes closest to truth and becomes authentically healing when surrendered to the power of the Holy Spirit. As a whole, the dove, creation, and Freud form the Cross of the Clinical Christ. Lord of Treatment, the Clinical Christ is the Sovereign into whose kingdom the practitioner of *Christian Holism* annexes all psychological theory and practice. On this cross, the Clinical Christ absorbs and destroys sin and psychopathology and radiates forth the restorative medicine of radical forgiveness and extreme sanity.

Cover Art Permissions

1. Michelangelo. The Sistine Chapel; ceiling frescos after restoration.
The Creation of Adam.
Sistine Chapel, Vatican Palace, Vatican State
Photo Credit: Erich Lessing/Art Resource, NY
2. Sigmund Freud: Freud Museum, London

Cover—Designed by King Design Group, LLC
    www.designisking.com

*Case Material regrading specific persons is used by permission.
Identifying information is altered to protect privacy.*

Published by:
Julian's House
Artistry with Words
Robin Caccese, BS, MT(ASCP)
137 Proudfoot Dr., Birdsboro, PA 19508
Phone: 610-582-5571; Fax: 610-582-7112; rcaccese@talon.net
www.christianhealingresources.org

Permissions

Grateful acknowledgement is made to all authors who gave permission for articles that they co-authored to be printed in this volume:

Robin Caccese, B.S., M.T.(A.S.C.P.)
Varuschka DeMarici, Psy.D.
Ronald J. Pekala, Ph.D.
Rev. Herman Riffel
James L. Schaller, M.D., M.A.R.
Douglas Schoeninger, Ph.D.
Julie Wegryn, M.S., M.A.T., N.C.C.

Grateful acknowledgements are also made to T. Harpur who gave permission for material from his book *The Uncommon Touch* to be quoted and HarperCollins for permission to quote material from *A Dictionary of Miracles* by E. Brewer.

Dedication
to
Julie Wegryn and Doug Schoeninger
and
the Healing Mission Team
Church of the Good Shepherd
Rosemont, PA

God bless you, my comrades
in divine arms.

Acknowledgement to Denise Manganelli
for her wonderful read through. Thanks!

Table of Contents

Foreword

Barbara Shlemon Ryan, RN
Be-loved Ministry

"I am certain that after the dust of centuries has passed over our cities, we, too, will be remembered not for victories or defeats in battle or in politics, but for our contribution to the human spirit." -- *John Fitzgerald Kennedy*

Dr. Charles Zeiders' writings stand as powerful contributions to the human spirit. In most of today's world the practice of modern psychology is severely handicapped by steadfastly separating body, mind, and spirit. His writings lift this veil of fear and misunderstanding by presenting a viable and effective alternative. Several years ago I was employed as a psychiatric nurse in a large Veteran's Administration hospital located in the Midwest. Group therapy sessions were scheduled each week with the intention of uncovering the underlying cause of the patients' mental problems. The clinical staff was instructed to discourage any discussions of spirituality during these gatherings because they presented an obstacle to recovery. It saddens me that I can recall very few lasting breakthroughs for those troubled souls. Dr. Zeiders refutes this form of therapy by demonstrating the beneficial effects of healthy spiritual experiences. He cites the copious amounts of scientific data that give strong arguments for the inclusion of spirituality in treatment plans. *The Clinical Christ* is a radical departure from today's demystified form of analytic psychiatry and psychology. The insights and examples gleaned from Dr. Zeiders' professional experience are sure to bring renewed hope to all who seek to discover true wholeness. I believe his writings will open the door to a fresh wind of the Holy Spirit in the mental health field.

Introduction

Charles L. Zeiders, Psy.D.

Psychologists can measure normalcy, define madness, develop therapeutic paradigms, and list the nuances of human nature with utmost precision. We have biofeedback, psychometrics, psychoanalysis, cognitive therapy, positive psychology, behavior modification, and a host of deeply promising projects in the research and development pipeline. To be sure, our discipline has advanced accurate understanding of the soul's essential properties and has scientifically harnessed this knowledge to clinically mitigate the deep agony of the human mind. But, despite our advances and genuine effectiveness, our discipline remains incomplete. Theoretically, scientifically, and therapeutically, we fall short of the fuller effectuality that awaits us. We need Christ.

It is through the Christian revelation that psychology will find its maturity. In our incorporation of the divine breakthrough recorded in the New Testament, our theories will become more true, because we will develop them in the light of Truth. Our therapies will become more powerful, because we will submit them to the source of Power. Our knowledge of human nature—as good but fallen, redeemed through Jesus, loved by a powerful, active triune God—will have tremendous impact on our disciplinary pursuits. Because God created humanity, all psychological science implicitly situates research data in relation to the creator. Because the sovereign God heals, we can submit our therapeutic interventions to his sovereignty and enjoy a therapy the nature of which is saturated by grace. Cognitive or dynamic interventions can become so imbued with divinity that the clinician's technique and the patient's receptivity uncannily unfold toward health. For psychology there are blessings afoot. And these blessings stem from our recognition that the Clinical Christ—the activity of the God of the Christian revelation throughout the realms of our discipline—desires to redeem, relate, heal, love, and empower us. The Clinical Christ seeks to bring us individually and corporately into a level of exuberant wholeness that is ultimately endless and utterly wonderful. The Clinical Christ is the Lord of the transformative psychology of *Christian Holism*. The chapters of this book explore different aspects of the Clinical Christ, *Christian Holism*, and their implications.

A group of colleagues and I have spent years experiencing the Clinical Christ in our practice of *Christian Holism*. From our spiritual/clinical experience, we felt an obligation to develop a theology of psychotherapy. Under the auspices of the Institute for Christian Counseling and Therapy, we formed the *Think Tank for Christian Holism*. The Think Tank consisted of three licensed psychologists, a minister and pastoral therapist, and an author and publisher of religious books—all practicing Christians and veterans of psychological and spiritual practice. From our efforts emerged the following tenets of Christian Holism:

The Central Tenet of Christian Holism is that the Holy Spirit is present and active during treatment.
Next:

- *Christian Holism is centered in Jesus Christ. The entire process of psychotherapy is explicitly under the Lordship of Jesus Christ. Treatment is conducted in His name.*
- *Christian Holism concerns itself with placing psychological theories and interventions at the disposal of the Holy Spirit.*
- *Christian Holism views the Hebrew and Christian scriptures, the Old and New Testaments, as inspired by the Holy Spirit, and a valid source of inspiration and guidance for psychotherapeutic treatment.*
- *Christian Holism thinks of creeds and catechisms as powerful statements of core beliefs, core convictions, which help to position the intellect in such a way that the entire person may develop openness to the presence and healing reality of God.*
- *Christian Holism is ecumenical.*
- *Christian Holism distinguishes itself as a psychological perspective in its conviction that men and women are made in the Image of God.*
- *Christian Holism facilitates reconciliation with God, with self, with those in the human community and creation.*
- *Christian Holism places social science under the Lordship of Jesus Christ. Under Christ's dominion, treatment relies on natural therapeutic processes and supernatural grace to accomplish healing.*
- *Christian Holism employs both "secular" (psychological and relational-ethical) and "sacred" (spiritual-biblical) interventions to participate in the Holy Spirit's Ministry to the client.*
- *Christian Holism is practiced by a therapist who provides sanctuary in which the client's healing process can unfold.*

If it is God's will, may *Christian Holism* inform your practice and guide your healing.

In *Christian Holism*, therapeutic forgiveness ranks among the most powerful clinical activities, and the Clinical Christ blesses such work with special healing favor. Jesus knows that our capacity to heal, communicate with God, and receive God's full blessing, greatly depends upon our capacity to forgive. That is why he tells us to forgive so we will be forgiven (Lk 6:37), to forgive others their trespasses (Mt 6:12), and to forgo our retribution requirements to a seemingly absurd degree (Mt 18:21-22). Research and scientific models bear out that unforgiveness is pathogenic: chronic anger adversely affects health (Kaplan, 1992); anger plays a role in decreased immune functioning (Herbert & Cohen, 1993); and stress from chronic unforgiveness imbalances the nervous system, causing physical and psychological problems (Newberg, d'Aquili, Newberg, deMarici, 2000). Conversely, forgiveness is curative: a growing body of research evidence points with increasing conclusivity that forgiveness positively correlates with measures of physical, psychological, and social health (Worthington, Berry, & Parrot, 2001). Plus, scientific and clinical evidence supports the position that forgiveness effectively treats a wide range of psychiatric disorders (Enright & Fitzgibbons, 2000). My own work in this area is based on a psychospiritual interpretation of Jesus' teaching in Mt 5:21-26. I find that my clients' *Will to Punish* those who have trespassed against them, imprisons them in the woundedness others inflicted upon them. When, through hard clinical work, these courageous people intentionally insert a *Will to Forgive* their trespassers over their *Will to Punish* them, the healing grace of God reaches the wounded portion of their soul and restores them. Sometimes the healing that follows forgiveness is dramatic, leaving clients in a euphoric state of grace with divinely inspired optimism. This predictable outcome of implementing the teachings of Jesus Christ, I have come to call *The Resurrection Effect*. (See p. 37 for a greater discussion of forgiveness, *The Resurrection Effect*, and the activity of the Clinical Christ.)

Christian spiritual psychology knows that forgiveness is the great healing deed of the Christian religion. When, through intense therapeutic effort and faith in God, a patient forgives, she heals. Similarly, shedding the alienating, pathogenic weight of sin by repentance and acceptance of the sacrifice of Jesus Christ, the health of reconciliation with God can be enjoyed. In fact, clinically and as a matter of theory, forgiveness appears to be a stepping stone to all types of reconciliation: reconciliation with self, others, and God. In my practice of *Christian Holism*, I have come to see that reconciliation itself is both a path and destination. As a path, reconciliation is moved forward in every corner of life by the God of love. As a destination, reconciliation is the end-game of the human condition and appears to be inexpressibly wonderful: To love and to be loved by God and to enjoy him forever. (See p. 69 for meditations on reconciliations.)

Dreams are another arena in which the Clinical Christ makes himself manifest. Therapeutically, dreams offer a wonderful corrective to a problem of human nature. During our tribulations, we sometimes cannot hear the wisdom of the greater parts of our soul, nor can we listen to the voice of God. But, just as God arranges his infinite consciousness into three persons to enjoy self reflection, the human spirit is similarly constructed. In dreams, the disparate aspects of our souls convene to converse and heal the whole person. Clinically, I have come to appreciate that dream activity occurs with the

Holy Spirit witnessing, understanding, and even arranging the dream. Dreams are charismatic gifts, given by the Holy Spirit to bless the individual and the Christian Community (Savary, Berne, & Williams, 1984). Interpreting a dream under the guidance of the Clinical Christ, a patient will place a hand upon his heart and—inspired by the dream's healing message—exclaim, like Jacob (Gen 28:16), "Surely God was in this place and I did not know it." (See p. 87 for an exploration of dreams and the Clinical Christ.)

An experience of energy sometimes accompanies prayers for Christian clients in the clinical setting. Pilgrims to holy sites like Medegordje or the Toronto Airport Church (original site of what is now known as the Toronto Blessing) often report that an energetic phenomenon accompanies their worship. Charismatics also experience divine energies moving through them and healing them. Just as God healed the hemorrhaging woman via the dynamic healing energy that flowed from Jesus (Mt 9:20-22; Mk 5:25-34; Lk 8:43-48), the Clinical Christ continues to offer his healing energy in the clinical arena at his discretion for our good. As a clinician, I find it moving how—at the concluding prayer of an intense therapeutic hour—I and my client sometimes feel the very energy of God palpably blessing, healing, and encouraging the patient forward with sensible, dancing power. (See p. 105 for an exploration of energy and the Clinical Christ.) Clinically, God's power can be felt.

Over the years, practicing *Christian Holism* and experiencing the healing activity of the Clinical Christ, I have come to appreciate God both as a person and as a clinical reality. Experiencing God as a person, I find that he wants my patients to heal, and wants me to be successful in helping them. God really cares and is clinically competent and wise and powerful. That is why in *Christian Holism*, Jesus is Lord of therapy, the Holy Spirit is clinically present, and the Father loves the enterprise. In the context of this reality, I find that God is an activist; that is, God does things that help the therapeutic process. God might inspire me to recall a long lost bit of psychodynamic theory which perfectly illuminates how a patient might heal, or God might answer a prayer for the healing of a chronic condition with such decisiveness that both I and my client struggle to understand the Trinity's loving use of power and gratuitous generosity. Experiencing God as a clinical reality, I have come to rely on him, as I do my cognitive-behaviorism. An empiricist, I have come to appreciate that scientific evidence exists to support the incorporation of prayer into the clinical setting. Not only that, but emerging science supports that notion that spiritual activity blesses people on a host of health-outcome indicators. Such science has import in the training of clinicians and even scientifically informs the Church, regarding how she might draw inspiration from social science to renew her own healing ministry with confidence. (Three chapters in this book examine these themes, beginning on p. 117.)

As you read this book, may God bless you with his truth and protect you from my errors. May God the Father, Son, and Holy Spirit be with you always—inspiring you by his dynamic presence and clinically empowering you to be an agent of his healing.

Charles L. Zeiders, Psy.D.
Licensed Psychologist
Chairman, *Think Tank for Christian Holism*
The Feast of *Corpus Christi*
Bryn Mawr, PA
2004

References

Enright, R., & Fitzgibbons, R., (2000). *Helping clients forgive.* Washington, D.C.: American Psychological Association.

Herbert, T., & Cohen, S. (1993). Stress and immunity in humans: a meta-analytic review. *Psychosomatic Medicine*, 50, 153-164.

Kaplan, B.H. (1992). Social health and the forgiving heart: The type B story. *Journal of Behavior Medicine*, 15, 3-14.

Newberg, A., d'Aquili, E., Newberg, S., & deMarici, V., (2000). The neuropsychological correlates of forgiveness. In M. McCullough, K. Paragament, & C. Thorsen (Eds), *Forgiveness: Theory, research, and practice* (pp. 91-110). New York: Guilford Press.

Savary, L., Berne, P., & Williams, S.K. (1984). *Dreams and spiritual growth: A Judeo-Christian way of dreamwork.* New York: Paulist Press.

Worthington, E., Berry, J., & Parrot, L. (2001). *Unforgiveness, forgiveness, religion, and health.* In Plante & A. Sherman (Eds.), *Faith and health: Psychological perspectives* (pp. 107-138). New York: The Guilford Press.

Tenets of *Christian Holism* for Psychotherapeutic Treatment

Charles L. Zeiders, Psy.D.
Douglas Schoeninger, Ph.D.
Rev. Herman Riffel
Robin Caccese, BS, MT(ASCP)
Julie Wegryn, MS, MAT, NCC

Christian Holism defines the place and work of the Holy Spirit in psychological counseling. *Christian Holism* is an emerging psychological perspective predicated on Christian principles. It is a transpersonal psychology that acknowledges the divinity of Christ. It strives to develop a practical way of thinking and working within psychological disciplines, while serving Christendom and its living God. *Christian Holism* seeks to enlist the blessings inherent in social science to the purpose of reclaiming the *Imago Dei* in persons. *Christian Holism* strives to retain flexibility to incorporate new, healthful science and theories about human nature, while keeping sturdy faith in the redemptive work of Jesus Christ operating in the clinical situation through the divine economy of the Holy Trinity.

S ince the mid 1970's, the Institute for Christian Counseling and Therapy has been developing a type of psychotherapy that incorporates elements of secular psychology firmly under the guidance of the Holy Spirit in the name of Jesus Christ. By the late '90's the clinicians reached consensus that the theory and practice of *Christian Holism* had become sufficiently mature to be developed into a set of principles or tenets for use by interested Christians, practitioners, and academics within the mental health professions. Dr. Zeiders developed prototypes of the tenets of *Christian Holism* and presented this list to the *Think Tank for the Development of Christian Holism*, comprised of members of the Institute for Christian Counseling and Therapy. For the year prior to the Fall/Winter, 2001 issue of the *Journal of Christian Healing*, the Think Tank convened under the Chairmanship of Dr. Zeiders to discuss the tenets, hone them, and propose more. Each Think Tank session focused on discussing a single tenet. Sessions were recorded and transcriptions were prepared. Think Tank members edited the transcripts and made additions. Dr. Schoeninger then edited the formal tenets into final form with

* This article was first published in *The Journal of Christian Healing*, Volume 22, #3&4, Fall/Winter, 2001, pp. 5-41.

the approval of the Think Tank. The authors listed above are the principals who share responsibility for pioneering and articulating this approach. Emerging from this labor is a Central Tenet of *Christian Holism* and ten additional tenets. Before adjourning, the Think Tank agreed that the tenets are far from complete. Much more needs to be done, especially in terms of developing tenets regarding how the redemptive work of Christ applies to the clinical enterprise and delineating a theory of psychopathology that is more explicitly Christian than current theories.

Listed first is the Central Tenet of *Christian Holism*, the most important idea for the governance of our theory and practice. Following the Central Tenet are ten additional tenets that guide our thinking regarding important areas of Christian mental health practice. Each tenet is presented in three segments: first, the formal edited tenet, second, initial commentary by Dr. Zeiders, and, third, relevant dialogue from Think Tank transcriptions.

The Central Tenet of *Christian Holism*

The Central Tenet of Christian Holism *for psychotherapeutic treatment is that the Holy Spirit is fully present in the clinical situation, with and within the therapist and the client(s), and is actively engaged in the treatment process.*

The Holy Spirit is completely present to the clinician and the client. The Holy Spirit is omnipresent, present everywhere and in every time of the client's life, without losing any particularity, and the Holy Spirit is omniscient, present to and discerning all realities—objective and subjective. The Holy Spirit works within and though the clinician and heals the client because the Holy Spirit honors the clinician and loves the client. The Holy Spirit works within the divine relatedness of the Holy Trinity, behaving toward the clinician and the client in an ongoing, person-loving way. The blessing of the Spirit's presence and activity unfolds both immediately and over time. The Holy Spirit is the prime mover of the healing process. The Holy Spirit acts with perfect and complete clinical competence, because the Holy Spirit is God's competence present with us.

Charles Zeiders: The Central Tenet is the most import idea that governs our therapy. The Spirit is in the midst of treatment and is therapeutically active. We know this because God loves us (Jn. 3:16). Naturally God wants us to do well—to find salvation, joy, and health. Thus, he sent Jesus. Jesus wants the good things that the Father wants for us (Jn. 8:28), so he sent the Spirit (Jn. 14:18). When clinicians and clients pray, the Spirit will gladly become present to them clinically. The Spirit of truth counsels the counseling. Then the benefits of the all-powerful, all-knowing, all-loving God become manifest in the midst of the clinical enterprise.

God is present everywhere. *Christian Holism* emphasizes this profundity. In this approach, the Holy Spirit is believed to be especially present when

The Central Tenet of *Christian Holism* for psychotherapeutic treatment is that the Holy Spirit is fully present in the clinical situation, with and within the therapist and the client, and is actively engaged in the treatment process.

invited by clinician and client to advance treatment in the name of Jesus Christ. The Spirit is ontologically present and helpful in the clinical situation. This is foundational.

Rev. Herman Riffel: The work of the Holy Spirit is primarily to make Jesus real to us.

Julie Wegryn: My experience in doing therapy is of the Holy Spirit directing and guiding, which is a little bit more than saying the Spirit is engaged in the process. I invite the Holy Spirit to direct and guide the process. I actively assume this and look to the Holy Spirit's direction. An example of this is the manifestation of the Holy Spirit's presence at times as an inner leading or an inner sense of guidance which does not fit any planned therapeutic intervention or comes at a time when the therapist has no idea of what to do. It may be guidance that the therapist would never have thought of in her usual patterns of therapeutic intervention.

Charles: And through this guidance the Holy Spirit works magnificently in terms of process. In the process people come to realize that their God is proactive, relevant, persistent and excitingly kind—always. The blessings of this process usually unfold over time. I say this because in my experience, while miracles do happen, they are statistically infrequent. I do not feel that we should make miracles the center of our focus, expecting them at every turn.

Doug Schoeninger: God's action is always holistic. The healing work of the Holy Spirit, God's work, is always in the context of the whole person and all the inter-relatedness within the whole person and between persons within the whole body of mankind, and most especially the immediate and generational context of the person. My experience is that most changes are developmental. They manifest gradually, as normal growth occurs. They develop over time in God's order etched into creation and moved and inhabited by his Spirit. This is both obvious and shocking. The Holy Spirit, the Spirit of the Father/Creator and of Jesus, this Spirit is the very mind and power of creation. Therefore, we are working with the author of the very whole that we are attempting to heal. So, the very mind that created us is the mind that is active in healing. The Holy Spirit is the intelligence that created all things, therefore grasps all things and is able to penetrate all things (Hebrews 4:9). To circle back to your words, Charles, the Holy Spirit is completely clinically competent.

Julie: And beyond that. Beyond any competence we can conceive. The Holy Spirit is beyond what we can imagine competence to be. That is why sometimes when we are listening to and allowing ourselves to be led by the Spirit we are moved to do things with the client that we would never have thought of doing, actions outside of our ordinary mode.

Charles: This leading to perform "actions outside our usual mode" can take the form of extraordinary clinical creativity and insight into a client's problems, such as uncanny intuition or suddenly saying exactly the right healing words. This fleshes out the concept that the Holy Spirit directs and guides the therapeutic process or *weaves* the process of the session.

Doug: Always, and always exceedingly exact, right, and novel at the same time. That is one of the outstanding qualities when you experience God's action. It is just right and yet surprising. God's action has both those aspects to it. Charles, you said it when you said, "People will realize that their God is proactive, relevant and excitingly, even, surprisingly kind."

I had a perfect illustration today of engaging the conviction inherent in this Central Tenet. I was with a woman who, given her brokenness and the circumstances of her life, is about to become homeless. She just has no place to go and, seemingly, her wounds prevent her from gaining access to resources that could benefit and lead her somewhere. She truly feels that her grown children do not want her to stay with them very long. She is in her mid 60s. So, it comes down to the question, "Is there anyone for her." All I could do with her was to stand for the reality that somehow her God is present and active for her. I do not have any solutions for her. God forbid, I am not even going to try to offer any. If the Holy Spirit inspires me, I will offer questions or suggestions. Her questions are, "Is there anyone to turn to? Is there anyone working on my behalf?" There is or there is not. These are very basic questions. What are we going to assume? That is the question I engaged with her. What are we going to assume?

Julie: This is right down to the bottom line.

Doug: Sometimes you are just at the bottom line with someone, with no answers except the faith that God is present for the person and actively engaged in providing for her welfare, somehow.

Charles: The therapist is a person who operates on behalf of the client with the understanding that regardless of external circumstances or degree of psychological problems, the Holy Spirit is operating on behalf of your client.

Doug: Yes, even the therapist cannot understand how the Spirit is going to act or manifest. The therapist cannot see any way out. The therapist holds the conviction that God is present and actively making provision on behalf of the client.

We might say that the Holy Spirit *is* complete competence, especially in situations such as these. The very same competent Spirit that brooded over the firmament (Genesis 1) broods over the therapeutic process.

The Holy Spirit is beyond
what we can imagine competence to be.

Robin Caccese: I love how the *Amplified* version of the Bible (1987) fleshes out this kind of action of the Holy Spirit in Genesis chapter one. It takes key scriptural words and puts in other possible meanings of the Hebrew text.

> In the beginning God (prepared, formed, fashioned, and) created the heavens and the earth. [Heb. 11:3] The earth was without form and an empty waste, and darkness was upon the face of the very great deep. The Spirit of God was moving (hovering, brooding) over the face of the waters (Gen. 1:1-3).

This is the first account of creation. The second account, beginning in Gen. 2:4 is also interesting in demonstrating some actions of the Holy Spirit in the therapeutic context.

> ... In the day that the Lord God made the earth and the heavens ... But there went up a mist (fog, vapor) from the land and watered the whole surface of the ground ... (vs. 6).

In the therapy process there are the times of darkness ... the dark waste ... or the formless void ... or the waters of chaos .... The action of the Holy Spirit in the therapy process does lots of *preparing, forming, fashioning* and there are often lots of tears ... *mists, fogs, vapors* watering the "whole surface of the ground." I also like the translation of Ps. 51:10 in *The Message* (Peterson, 1995):

> "God, make a fresh start in me,
> shape a Genesis week from the chaos of my life."

These are such good metaphors for the action of the Holy Spirit in the therapeutic process.

Charles: So, the mind that created the universe is the mind that is active, brooding over us, in restoring and healing the client. The Holy Spirit is the prime mover of treatment, the ultimate therapeutic force and completely clinically competent ...

Doug: ... and is the primary and ultimate healing force and intelligence.

Robin: The Holy Spirit is beyond methodologies and definitions, even our best definition of integration. God has a bigger and higher and wider and deeper and vaster definition of integration than we could possibly articulate.

Herman: And further, in the case of physical miracles, they may be perfectly real and good, but when you look at the whole picture of the person, perhaps the person has only received the physical healing. There may be much more that has not yet been healed. The physical miracle may not have encompassed all the healing the person needs.

Robin: And, looking at it the opposite way, if a physical miracle does not happen when you pray, perhaps you may have missed other subtle things that have happened and been healed. A concept of holism suggests holding the whole picture.

Charles: Yes, think also about the analogy of prayer as water. If you plant a seed and water it, it does not appear to grow immediately. Immediate apparent growth would be miraculous. Prayer is a way of watering the soul, and it causes the spiritual genetic code that God has placed in the soul to unfold its process according to God's design.

Herman: What I'm so impressed with constantly as I meet various groups is the fact of the necessity that we need to be always open to what the Holy Spirit is doing and calling us to see. We never come to a place where we've *got it* because as soon as we think we do, we have put a limited human framework around God.

Tenets Proceeding from the Central Tenet

1. Christian Holism *is centered in Jesus Christ. The entire process of psychotherapy is explicitly under the Lordship of Jesus Christ. Treatment is conducted in His name.*

Charles: *Christian Holism* is centered in Jesus Christ, because "Christ is Lord of the cosmos and of history" (*Catechism of the Catholic Church*, 1994, p. 191). Since Christ is Lord of all things, therapy is authentically ordered when our therapeutic service is under Christ's dominion. Clinically, we find that Christ enjoys helping patients, because he cares for them so much. Jesus of Nazareth brought good news to the afflicted, liberty to captives, sight to the blind, freedom to the oppressed, and proclaimed God's favor (Lk. 4:18-19). Made Lord of treatment, Jesus continues to do these kind things by sending his Spirit to those treated.

Herman: To conduct therapy in Jesus' name means to follow him. This is a response to a person (Jesus) by a person. Therefore following him does not always look the same, certainly for different persons. For example, in my youth I responded to an altar call to give my life to Jesus and nothing seemed to happen to me. Apparently there were certain *other* steps that I personally was to take to come to Jesus. Later, during a time my father was praying for me, I suddenly had the experience of being born again. Coming to the experience of being born again in this way, did not fit into the framework of my church's thinking and its explicit traditions and expectations. Taking this notion further, many from my Mennonite background do not feel that Catho-

The Holy Spirit is beyond methodologies and definitions, even our best definition of integration. God has a bigger and higher and wider and deeper and vaster definition of integration than we could possibly articulate.

lics are Christian, because they have not followed all the *right* steps. As it is, I have learned that Catholics have their own steps.

Charles: You just helped me realize something that is going to flesh out this Tenet. Under the Lordship of Jesus Christ, the Holy Spirit will move within understood paradigms and the Holy Spirit will move in ways that seem outside of known paradigms, at the Lord's pleasure for the good of the person.

Doug: According to the Lord's love for that person.

Charles: To me working under the Lordship of Jesus means, first off, power of attorney. In *Christian Holism* therapists are operating on behalf of a sovereign person, utilizing powers that are given to them under the sovereign's authority. At the same time the therapists recognize that they are not the author of the authority that they exercise. It also implies that by misusing the authority that they are given in Jesus' name, they corrupt the entire enterprise, which is not good for the client, the therapist, or God.

Herman: Working under Jesus' Lordship also implies exercising responsibility. We are given basic direction from Jesus, through the Spirit and through the written word, our scriptures, but we are also expected to understand and be able to interpret that which is given to us. What is given to us may be an essence, a basic principle. We then have to work out the basic principle. In that working it out, we have to learn how to relate to others in their interpretations. Working in Jesus' name is like being an ambassador for a country. You speak for that country and you represent that country with authority even though you speak in your own words.

Doug: You are working under delegated authority.

Herman: Yes.

Robin: I think part of the working out that is involved is learning how to apply Jesus' direction and authority in different situations.

Doug: Clarify for me, Herman, what you mean by *principle* because being under the Lordship of Jesus is not being under the Lordship of a principle. It's the Lordship of a person, so I see myself as operating under the authority of a person who is active.

Herman: In the scripture we feel that God is speaking to us, but we have to learn how to apply it, as Robin said. There is going to be a difference of interpretation between people, while at the same time, both are under the Lordship of Christ.

Doug: So you are saying we take responsibility for living this out, for interpreting our own integrity in being under authority in the moment. At the same time we respect others' interpretations, those of persons we are working with as clients or as colleagues, who are also doing their best to interpret the Lordship of Christ in the moment.

Herman: And this awareness gives us a responsibility towards others, because he is Lord, not only of me, but he is Lord for the other, and we have to respect that, and somehow discern together.

Robin: Before going further, I want to surface the fact that I do not relate very well to this phrase, "The Lordship of Jesus." It sounds too distant. What I imagine when I am praying with somebody is that Jesus is beside me, and I imagine myself leaning toward him, kind of like with my ear to the source. I am not thinking in terms of Lordship. That sounds too cool and distant.

Doug: How, then, do you relate to Jesus' authority? How is Jesus' authority active in the way that you work?

Robin: The only thing I work with is an image of my ear pressed to the heart and the mouth of Jesus.

Doug: If you are interpreting Jesus through what you sense or what you see through the vehicle of your imagination, and you are in dialogue with Jesus and you follow Jesus, wouldn't that be Jesus' Lordship in operation.

Robin: Oh, I follow your thought.

Doug: You do not lead him.

Robin: Oh no.

Doug: He leads you. That is the point I was trying to make. What I am saying is that you experience an immediacy of Jesus' Lordship, because - yes, you are companions—but you are not there as equals, so you do not assume an equal authority. You do not say, "Forget it. My way is better. Go back to your drawing board, Jesus."

Robin: Oh no. I would not even attempt to do that!

Doug: So there is order to the relationship.

Robin: I never even think in those ways, Doug.

Doug: I hear that you don't, but, on the other hand, you may operate in those ways while not using those terms. You take your lead and direction from Jesus.

Charles: I think I understand what you are saying, Robin. The way you hear the term *Lordship* flashes you back to negative authority figures in your experience.

Robin: Yes, especially my father, and I did not want to be under his lordship because it was abusive.

Charles: So *Lordship* has connotations that come out of the misuse of parental authority in your family and also, I suspect, your experience with misuses of ecclesiastical authority.

Robin: Yes, the word *Lordship* has a negative tone to me, more like *lord-*

The way you hear the term *Lordship* flashes you back to negative authority figures in your experience.

ing over. I do not think of Jesus as *lording over* me.

Charles: As I think further about this reality of the Lordship of Jesus, I realize that I am also thinking about this realty in Trinitarian terms. As Christian therapy is taking place, it participates in the life of God the Father, the Son and the Holy Spirit. I think that I experience the Holy Spirit as providing power and direction and healing and gifting and moving the therapy in a direction. I experience Christ as making it possible to have access to his Spirit. Clinically, I think of it sort of as a Pentecostal experience, as when the early church became empowered and developed its gifting and received its orders from Christ through the Holy Spirit. I see Jesus Christ in his Lordship giving me the assignment to operate in his name and making it possible to avail myself clinically of the power of the Holy Spirit on behalf of my patient.

I may have gotten tangential. Let's refocus.

Robin: What was your original question about the Lordship? How did you phrase that?

Doug: "*Christian Holism* has a high Christology. The entire process of psychotherapy is explicitly under the Lordship of Jesus Christ. Treatment is conducted in his name." What does it mean to engage in a process that is under the Lordship of Jesus Christ?

Robin: The word that comes to me now is "direction." Now I think, Charles, you would put that in the realm of the Holy Spirit, but I am not thinking of listening to the Holy Spirit. I am thinking of listening to Jesus and the word that works for me is "direction," under the direction of Jesus.

Doug: So it means receiving direction and looking for direction.

Robin: And earnestly seeking it out and petitioning and interceding for direction.

Herman: But that is only part of it.

Doug: Well that is the part that Robin is relating to.

Herman: I mean not only listening and getting direction, but, then, speaking the word.

Doug: As a representative of Jesus.

Herman: As a representative. So you get your direction, and then you speak the word.

Doug: I am very cautious about that aspect. However, I can think of a number of times when I have had a sense to actually verbalize what I was perceiving Jesus saying to the person and actually standing in as Jesus voice. Most often I would turn to the person and ask them to tell me what they were hearing Jesus speak to them or seeing him doing. But there are times when I feel moved to speak as Jesus, thereby being a catalyst to the person opening up to their own listening and seeing. Sometimes my speaking seems an embodiment of Jesus' presence speaking and it is very fruitful. It seems to open the person to an experience of the presence of Jesus.

Robin: I recently made a leap of this sort when I conducted my first *Theophostic* (see: www.theophostic.com) prayer ministry session. I directed this session completely out of that listening and speaking mode. It was astonishing to me how my decision to let go of my anxiety that I might *do the technique wrong* and flow completely with what I sensed Jesus wanted me to do and say, bore fruit in the person's experience of deep healing.

Doug: So when we are treating in his name there is this representative piece. I am not there just as myself. I am there as myself, but I am there also as someone who is listening to, responding to, orienting to, drawing from the authority of, acting in the authority of, the one who sent me, Jesus. This is interesting in terms of the identity of the therapist. The identity of the therapist, as well as the process itself, flows from this being under and in the authority of Jesus and, therefore representing him.

Herman: I think I am hearing what you are saying. In order to choose to be a representative, a conduit of Jesus, one has to risk. In other words being a representative is a concept that one may respond to inwardly, but to actually live it out means taking a risk with what one receives.

Doug: If I am receiving direction and taking a risk with the direction that I perceive, just as one would take a risk with an intuition, I am accepting that my prayer is effective and that the senses and intuitions that are coming have some validity in the Spirit. I am risking that there is direction coming from Jesus and that I am following that direction to some degree. It is not going to be an incarnate moment, and it is not going to be in his name without the human risk of embodying the direction received in some way. Of course inward listening requires humility. It is I, imperfect, who am listening and hearing and responding. And speaking out of listening requires wisdom, attention to the whole person to whom I am speaking.

Charles: This all gets back to the point that to be a practitioner of *Christian Holism* is not simply a sort of craven collapse before the Lord—as a nothing—and not taking risks and that sort of thing. What it really demands of the practitioner is not simply faith, but also courage to operate in that faith, because in our lack of perfection, there is always the fear that we are doing something ridiculous and absurd rather than hearing the voice of God. So if we are really going to take the idea seriously—the idea that we are operating under the Lordship of Jesus Christ—then we have to have a level of faith that he really is our Lord and the Lord of the session and that he is going to intervene. Acting on the idea that Jesus is going to intervene requires courage as much as faith.

In order to choose to be a representative, a conduit of Jesus, one has to risk. In other words being a representative is a concept that one may respond to inwardly, but to actually live it out means taking a risk with what one receives.

Robin: Another thought just came to me. We can judge our effectiveness by the measurable fruitfulness that we can see in the person that we are working with.

Doug: "By their fruit you shall know them" (Matt. 7:16). By the fruits of our action we shall know that it was authentic action. Of course, it is not that easy, always, to measure fruitfulness, because results may not appear immediately or without struggle.

Robin: My experience has been with people in brief times of prayer, about one and a half hours, and they came to peace with an area of their lives that had been in conflict for a long time. Now this peace may have been short-lived (this will take follow up to ascertain), but the end point that we reached in this short time was very, very peaceful and then laughter commenced. The process seemed fruitful.

Charles: Yes and in the special moments to which you are referring, one can already see healing occurring. There is something special that has happened in the soul, and I think that what you were witnessing there is what I would call the *Resurrection Effect*. I see it in the process of forgiveness, but I do not think the *Resurrection Effect* is limited to forgiveness. The *Resurrection Effect* is the outcome of a healing process happening successfully and, by successfully, I mean in a way that Jesus really likes.

Robin: At times it is simply a matter of standing there with a person as the person asks for prayer and then continuing to stand there, praying in tongues and perhaps just touching the person's forehead or shoulder. There were moments in that *Theophostic* session to which I just referred where I felt that we were at a stuck point, and I just had the sense to put my hand on the person's head as a means of giving them a sense of touch. I was doing this in the name of Jesus, and it seemed to help move the healing process.

Doug: When you said, "I'm doing this in the name of Jesus" what did you mean?

Robin: My experience was of my hand becoming Jesus' hand. I did not say that to the person, but that is what I felt.

Doug: For me taking a risk like this, of being Jesus for the other, is balanced by a sense of fragility in taking the risk. In a moment I may feel confident or I may not feel confident, but the fact of the matter is that as human beings we must take risks to embody Jesus. On the other hand, there is always the risk that we are missing the mark, misunderstanding Jesus. You cannot take a risk knowing for sure that you are accurately representing Jesus. You take the risk and then trust the Holy Spirit to continue to work with you and the other.

Charles: Yes. Courage is required.

Doug: One of the tendencies in attempting to exercise the gift of listening to God is ego inflation. One can get too certain that what one hears or senses is God speaking. Then one begins to speak in a definite manner, "This is what God is saying," as opposed to, "This is what I hear. Would you like to hear it?" or "Here's what I hear. What do you hear?"

Herman: Yet there are times when the word to be spoken does require a declaration, not a qualification.

Doug: Yes. However, I am not speaking of a rule or an absolute regarding the form of speech. I am pointing to an attitude. The form may be directly stated, declared, because that is the sense of the intuition you have at the moment. For example one senses God saying, "I love you. I am embracing you," and declares it just like that. However, inwardly one can question the source without deflating the movement. It is a matter of knowing one is human.

Charles: We have been talking about Jesus as the Lord of the therapy. We hear the voice of the Lord, and our mission is to articulate his voice as we hear it as part of the therapy. When we do this, we need to bring a character virtue into play, which is humility. I think this is worth exploring, because it is that character virtue that is going to buffer and vaccinate the therapist against the possibility of his own psychopathology being confused with the authentic voice of Jesus. Humility prevents us from getting narcissistically caught up.

Doug: When I speak in Jesus' name, I want to be sure I have heard him, but I am not certain. Qualitatively, I will feel a warmth. I will feel a sense of the word to be spoken. I will feel something, which I experience to be in the character of Jesus. I have internalized images of Jesus that have grown from the word in scripture and the warmth and sense in me meets those criteria, and so I speak, at the time, in an authoritative tone. At the same time, there is an aspect of me that is not certain, so I am willing to yield what I have spoken at any moment if it seems to be not fruitful or destructive or ill timed.

Robin: I have learned a technique that helps me with my spiritual director. If she asks me a question, and I am having difficulty relating to the question. I ask her if she can phrase the question in another way. Doing this both activates and counts on humility in her.

Herman: I would like to mention something that has been said in a way. This matter of the Lordship of Christ is not just a doctrinal position or a theoretical thing. We can say that we believe, but it is only an intellectual assent, that is, the mind agrees to it but the heart, or the whole self, is not with it. To believe demands action. It is well illustrated in the well-known

Agnes Sanford said, "As long as you say, 'God can help you,' it's all theory. It's only when you can say, 'I can help you,' that it is real." Only when I can say, "I know that I can pray the prayer of faith for you," has true practice begun.

story of the man who drove his wheelbarrow on a rope over Niagara Falls. The crowds cheered and believed he could do it again. But when he asked one of the "believers" to step into the wheelbarrow, the person did not believe anymore. Faith demands action. Recently I heard a British Pentecostal preacher illustrate this point while speaking to priests at a conference. He said he was praying for a blind man who had something wrong with his eyes. As he prayed, he had the impression that the Lord was giving him the healed eyes of the blind man. The test came to put action to his faith for that is often where we get stuck. He said, "It was necessary for me to put my hands up to his eyes (believing that the eyes healed) and declare it." If he believed what God had told him, he had to act on it.

Doug: To actually declare a reality ….

Charles: Did he do it?

Herman: Yes he did and the man had new eyes.

Doug: There are times when it is not an abstraction, aren't there? Jesus' authority is active. It is to be engaged.

Herman: That is right, and I think that we ought to make that clear. I think that there is a lot to the Lordship of Jesus Christ. Oh yes, we believe in the Lordship of Christ, but often for many of us that belief is all theory.

Charles: Herman you came up with a good example. The Lordship of Jesus Christ may mean that when you hear Jesus within your soul telling you to tell a blind man that his eyes are going to heal, you have got to declare it!

Herman: Agnes Sanford said, "As long as you say, 'God can help you,' it's all theory. It's only when you can say, 'I can help you,' that it is real." Only when I can say, "I know that I can pray the prayer of faith for you," has true practice begun.

Doug: That comes from an inner compulsion, an inner conviction.

Herman: Yes it does, but it also comes from an inner experience with Christ so that then it does not come as something one is trying to produce.

Doug: Well you have knowledge from your own relationship with Christ. But also, in the moment, you have a particular movement of faith, don't you? Agnes is not talking about faith as an abstraction. She is talking about faith as an active movement in the moment. "You have faith for," means you *do* have faith for it.

Charles: Herman, you made me realize that I am a better theoretician than a practitioner.

Herman: Well, that is what we are working to improve.

Charles: You have also contributed to my humility.

Herman: Humility is simply honesty, just like pride is lying.

Doug: Thank you, Herman. I am hearing two facets that *in his name* conveys, a facet of authority, an active authority, an authority that has to be not only embraced but ...

Robin: Lived.

Doug: Right, enacted, expressed. And the other word that comes to me is *shape*. *In his name* gives shape to the direction of healing or the direction of ministry in that Jesus is the *shape* of God. Jesus is the enfleshed character of God, the incarnate character of God.

Robin: He is the image of the unseen God.

Doug: Yes, so there is also shape, image to work from. It is like getting to know a person. You take the person within yourself, are shaped by the person, and you respond from the way in which you have internalized that person. That person has taught you. That person has given you wisdom. That person has ministered love to you. That which you have received you can give.

Charles: Here is another point about conducting treatment in Jesus' name (or praying for that matter). Some of the times when we pray, the prayers are not effective. That is because, while we are outwardly saying "in Jesus' name," we are inwardly saying "in my name." We are trying to get what we want and accidentally fall into an occultist trap. Bad faith may compromise the outcome, because Jesus really has not been Lord of treatment or my heart.

Doug: Or even if the outcome is God's will, my intent is not for the right reasons. My prayer is not an act of love. It is an act of my own desire, an act of power or control.

Charles: Well, maybe God and I have similar goals, but I have not made God Lord of the process. God might want my patient to be healed, but I might misguidedly look for it to be instantaneous. God might say, "No, in three weeks this lonely guy you are treating is going to meet a girl, and his depression is going to go into remission. Wait until then." So, to submit to God's *process*, I think, is as important as submitting to God's *goals*. If we were perfectly operating in our practices and in our lives in Jesus' name, everything that we would do, would be reflective of our internal posture of submission and our therapeutic activity would spring from that submission to Christ.

Doug: That depth of authority, of faith, which needs to be cultivated, may not have deepened to that level, to where you can say, "Mountain, move" and it will move. That is scriptural, but who has the experience, the authority, and the level of abandonment to Jesus, to say that?

Robin: In symbolic terms we have all experienced that authority. In

Rather than ask, "How do I intellectually integrate my training in social science with Christian doctrine?" the practitioner of *Christian Holism* asks, "How does the Holy Spirit want to use my training to help this client?"

working with a client you may be the one who has to speak to that mountain in their life that needs to be moved.

Doug: That is right, but in our culture I have been raised to view material reality, physical "mountains," as impenetrable to Spirit.

Robin: In the Newtonian worldview, perhaps, but the new Physics is opening up new thought, especially about the effectiveness of spirituality and prayer.

Doug: I am amazed when there is a physical healing. I am not as amazed when there is a psychological shift. Others would say that physical healing is simple. Pray, and it moves. For them, it is the psychological and the spiritual that are difficult. If the physical moves, I am surprised. If the psychological moves, I say, "Yes, I kind of know how that happened." It is magnificent, but I have a thought process for it. I have been schooled that the material is more powerful than the Spirit. That is the world I grew up in. It is probably exactly the opposite in truth, but there are levels of authority that are not operative in me for physical healing, because of the depth of that split in my consciousness.

2. Christian Holism *concerns itself with placing psychological theories and interventions at the disposal of the Holy Spirit.*

Rather than ask, "How do I intellectually integrate my training in social science with Christian doctrine?" the practitioner of Christian Holism *asks, "How does the Holy Spirit want to use my training to help this client?" In* Christian Holism, *placing social science at the disposal of the living God is the paramount concern that trumps problems of theoretical integration.*

Charles: Accomplishing scholarship that integrates psychological theories with Christian theology is important, but the mission of *Christian Holism* calls for asking God to quicken therapeutic skills and theories to bless those called to our offices. If our secular orientations are cognitive-behavioral, Jungian, etc., we ask God to bless those skills and theories in a way that makes the truth in them useful in the course of God's healing action. While religious faith cannot substitute for clinical skill, neither can clinical skill find wholeness or manifest its deeper therapeutic value without being graced by the God who wants to bless our clients utterly.

Christian Holism encourages exploring diverse approaches to healing under the guidance of the Holy Spirit. Healing practices from other cultures such as yoga, meditation, Qigong, and Reiki, as well as radical emerging therapies like breath work, Therapeutic Touch, and energy medicines are seen as potentially useful and potentially revealing of ways in which God made living beings. Nothing exists to prevent the Spirit from arranging our thinking about and use of various healing systems in a way that pleases God and blesses our clients (see Fabricant & Schoeninger, 1987 and Sears, 1999). God is as sovereign over Biblical Counseling as over yoga, Therapeutic Touch, and Thought Field Therapy. Truth from any of these healing practices has a place in the Kingdom of God and in *Christian Holism*.

Christian Holism is more concerned with service to Christ, integration into Christ, rather than with integration of secular psychological knowledge with Christian faith and doctrine. The concept or goal of integration can be a head-trip. For example, an integration question is, "How can I marry cognitive-behaviorism to Christianity?" One can do that, but this is not the essential focus of *Christian Holism*. Rather, centering in the Lordship of Jesus one might ask, "How does God wish to use my cognitive-behavioral expertise for his healing purposes now?" You could just as easily ask, "How does God want to use my muscle testing? How does God want to use my understanding of Analytical psychology? How does God want to use my rich theological training for his purposes now?" So, while *Christian Holism* is concerned with integration of secular and revealed knowledge, what we are more concerned with is putting the things developed in the secular world, or even in other religious systems, under Jesus' Lordship for his use.

Doug: We could say also, "What is the truth that God is revealing in this?" God is revealing all the time, so what is the truth God is revealing in this or that methodology or theory or research study, the truth for this situation and this person?

Herman: I am reminded of a young doctor in Australia who asked me, "How do you define schizophrenia?" I said, "I don't have to define schizophrenia. That is your term. The man is sick and he needs healing." I do not mean that it is not important to know what is understood in psychology and psychiatry about schizophrenia. However, we cannot be held to those definitions. We are listening to God regarding the healing of this person, and regarding how we understand any clinical condition.

Charles: You are saying that you are not treating a diagnosis. You are treating a child of God.

Doug: Placing knowledge under the Lordship of Jesus means that a particular conception of schizophrenia is used as God reveals it, in a way that helps us to know how to help a person or a type of person. We annex the truthfulness of health theories and techniques. God reveals God's self and ways in secular knowledge and technique. God reveals God's self within the created order. When we annex ideas of social science and other healing paradigms, we are not annexing something that is alien to God. We are annexing

God reveals God's self and ways in secular knowledge and technique. God reveals God's self within the created order. When we annex ideas of social science and other healing paradigms, we are not annexing something that is alien to God.

that which reveals the nature of God and the nature of God's creation. We do not integrate knowledge in the sense of trying to put everything into Christian terms. We see the truth revealed in a piece of psychoanalytic theory or Jungian theory or whatever. And it may, of course, get re-mapped and re-shaped as we allow Jesus to work it into our schema.

Robin: Because the bottom line is that, "If you abide in my word, you shall be my disciples indeed, and you shall know the truth, and the truth shall make you free" (John 8:32)

3. Christian Holism *views the Hebrew and Christian scriptures, the Old and New Testaments, as inspired by the Holy Spirit, and a valid source of inspiration and guidance for psychotherapeutic treatment.*

Therefore, scripture is useful to guide case formulations and interventions. While scripture reveals truth, interpretations are, of course, colored by human imperfection. Hence, when utilizing scripture to guide treatment, the clinician must exercise theological humility. Read in humility, under the Spirit's guidance, scripture assists the psychological enterprise by shedding light on how God improves the health of patients. In Christian Holism, *scripture is used to help reveal God's healing movements, as led by the Holy Spirit. Scripture is an anointed resource, a rich, unique medium for God's guidance and personal address of the client and therapist.*

Charles: "Sacred scripture must be read and interpreted in the light of the same Spirit by whom it was written" (*Catechism of the Catholic Church, 1994, p. 37-38*). In terms of *Christian Holism,* this means that scripture is most therapeutic when the Spirit is invited to inspire textual meaning in light of the Spirit's healing ministry to the client. Further, while scripture has both collective and individual significance, the Spirit arranges these meanings in the minds of both client and clinician in ways that offer hope and promote health. Because scripture reveals truth about God and man, scripture is revered. However, as Herman Riffel notes below, *Christian Holism* carefully avoids idolizing scripture, reserving worship only for the God who inspires revelation and healing through the faith's documents.

Read in humility, under the Spirit's guidance, scripture assists the psychological enterprise by shedding light on how God improves the lot of man and offers guidance for the specific persons in treatment. In my experience of using scripture in treatment, I find a creative dialectic between scripture and psychological theory. Reading scripture through the lens of social science and reading social science through the lens of scripture opens up treatment options and understandings.

Herman: This dialectic occurred for me when I was studying at the Jung Institute in Zurich, Switzerland. Looking at salvation and sanctification from the viewpoint of Jung's concept of individuation opened a whole depth realm in my understanding of conversion. I began to see depths and dimensions to the deep inner self growing in Christ. I also began to see that Jesus worked out in himself the full balance in the human personality and is offering us the power of his incarnation through the work of the Holy Spirit in us.

Charles: This creative interaction of psychodynamic awareness and spiritual insight occurs not only in my consciousness, but also for clients as they allow scripture to evoke self-awareness. They then experience the meaning of the scripture, enlarged through understanding how different parts of their personality react to the scriptural word. For example, reading the beatitudes in Matthew chapter five puts persons in touch with a variety of inner reactions, both believing and cynical—or even despairing. Then working therapeutically with these various reactions or parts within the personality can bring more of the client into touch with God's transforming grace.

Herman: I want to emphasize, however, that scripture is the map and not the territory or the substance. Where is your bible? [Herman, holding up a bible] This is not *the* Word of God. It contains in it, written words about *the* Word of God.

Doug: Do you mean that scripture expresses our experience of God? It is a community's text, spiritually inspired and inspiring. It is not *the* Word itself. The text is not God.

Herman: The bible is inspired. We recognize that it is God that we are worshipping—who is revealed in our bible. I mention this, because, when we discuss scripture, we speak of scripture as the word of God. We can subtly begin to deify scripture. Scripture is inspired and unique and puts into human language, God's expression. However, God is God and Jesus is the living Word of God. Engaging the Word of God means, to me, engaging the living Jesus Christ, which of course scripture helps me do in a unique and inspired way.

4. Christian Holism *views creeds and catechisms similarly to the way it views scripture.* Christian Holism *thinks of creeds and catechisms as powerful statements of core beliefs, core convictions, which help to position the intellect in such a way that the entire person may develop openness to the presence and healing reality of God. In* Christian Holism, *creeds and catechisms are not end points but points of opening toward the God of healing, and to the dimensions of God's presence to us as Father, Son and Holy Spirit.*

While deeply respecting the creeds, *Christian Holism* holds that people are loved by God—not due to creedal affiliations— but because people are made in the *Imago Dei* and God simply loves people.

Charles: *Christian Holism* appreciates that creeds and catechisms preserve central ideas about the Christian faith and reality. When the Holy Spirit makes them instruments of healing—such as by positioning the discouraged intellect to conceptualize God's love and anticipate healing grace—creeds and catechisms become therapeutically practical. *Christian Holism* also appreciates that Christians and others will hold varying conceptions of Christianity and reality in good faith. While deeply respecting the creeds, *Christian Holism* holds that people are loved by God—not due to creedal affiliations— but because people are made in the *Imago Dei* and God simply loves people. The therapeutic purpose of creeds is to open clients to God's healing love and to create an open place in the mind that can be inhabited by the felt experience of Trinity.

For me, *Christian Holism* adheres to the essential Christian doctrines embodied in the creeds. I am referring to the Nicene creed and the Apostles creed. I know that historically the church was aware of the need to have a bottom line, core beliefs. It is great to have the freedom of the Holy Spirit, which our earlier tenets discuss, but there is also a bottom line and that is doctrine, core belief. The Apostles creed is regarded as the formulation of the essential convictions of the Christian faith. The Nicene creed asserts the truth and integrity of the Trinity. For me these things are not up for grabs. We worship a triune God, three in one. We can have other things as peripherals but this statement is bedrock belief. I do my therapy with these conceptual tools in mind.

Herman: To me it looks like this: the creeds are near the ground level, but underneath are the roots going down and if there is any bottom line it is in Christ. We are constantly drawing from that great creative root.

Doug: Are you saying that the creeds themselves are pointing to a deeper mystery unfolding? The creeds are our best attempt to articulate the mystery? The mystery itself is the reality of Jesus Christ?

Herman: I am just saying that having these two creeds is great, but they do not satisfy me as far as the mystery of God is concerned. We might say that they are the filters that we come through in reaching for our root. We are reaching into Christ.

Charles: Nor do the creeds exhaust the mystery. The creeds point us towards the living reality of God and God's nature.

Doug: The creeds are our, the church's, attempt to articulate the mystery,

Clinical ecumenism allows the healing goodness inherent in the gifts of each of the churches to enter therapy at the Spirit's pleasure. Clinical ecumenism opens treatment to the universe of spiritual gifts contained within the entire body of Christ. By acknowledging that the Spirit-given gifts of competing communities complement each other and belong together, the small clinical situation contributes to healing dissociation within the larger church situation.

---

the basic Tenets of that mystery, but in no way contain the mystery.

Herman: The main thing I would say again is that the creeds express our understanding, but there is still more that we need to look at. Our roots are still in Christ.

Charles: What is important to me therapeutically is that adhering to the creeds helps me, and then my clients, to open up to the resources available in God. For example the Nicene creed articulates the conviction that God relates to us in three manifestations, in a Trinitarian way, as Father, creator and restorer of the original plan; Jesus who makes things right between us and God, reconciler; and Holy Spirit, immediate presence, power, helper, teacher, and guide. God relates to us in these three ways. When I think of my experience of the healing manifestations of Trinity, I think of my experience of awesome glory emanating from the Father, powerful acceptance from Jesus, and warm, purposeful, electrical charge from the Holy Spirit and a feeling of complete unreserved love between the Three into which I am invited. The Holy Spirit wants to share all of this life with us, especially the tremendous love and devotion between Father and Son.

Doug: Then the clinician rooted in the expectancies nurtured in the creeds, can be an active catalyst helping the client access these manifestations of God for his or her growth and healing.

5. Christian Holism *is ecumenical. There are two reasons for this.*
a)   *First, all Christian churches (or ecclesial communions) have valuable practices that can enter, or be availed, in the therapy situation to allow the Holy Spirit healing opportunities. Clinical ecumenism allows the healing goodness inherent in the gifts of the different ecclesial communions to enter therapy at the Spirit's pleasure, according to the client's healing need.*
b)   *Second, since The church is one body containing multiple and often competing units of organizational authority, the human, organized*

church is dissociated. Psychotherapeutic ecumenism honors the essen-
tial unity of The church and works to heal the dissociation of the human,
organized church within the clinical microcosm.

Charles: Catholic and Orthodox Churches, for example, impart the Spirit's grace through sacraments. Evangelical churches do this through emphasis on revealed truth and ethical responsibility, Quakers through contemplative listening, Pentecostals through charismatic experience, etc. Clinical ecumenism allows the healing goodness inherent in the gifts of each of the churches to enter therapy at the Spirit's pleasure. Clinical ecumenism opens treatment to the universe of spiritual gifts contained within the entire body of Christ. By acknowledging that the Spirit-given gifts of competing communities complement each other and belong together, the small clinical situation contributes to healing dissociation within the larger church situation.

To concretize the diverse and valuable giftedness worked out in the various communions, we could go on to talk about the healing value of the sacraments in Catholicism and Orthodoxy, the emphasis on revealed truth and ethical responsibility in evangelical Christianity, the importance of listening to God in Quakerism, and the efficacy of charismatic experience among Pentecostal denominations.

Robin: That is a nice list.

Charles: There are two reasons that I have been able to discern as to why *Christian Holism* needs to be ecumenical. One is that all the Christian ecclesial communions have healing charisms that bring us into the process of the reclamation of the *Imago Dei*, God's image in us. Two, psychotherapeutic ecumenism honors the unity of *the* church which is one body by working to heal the dissociation in the organized body. St. Paul says the body is a unit, which is made up of many parts and, though all of the parts are many, they form one body. So it is with Christ. We are the body of Christ, and the theologies, the doctrines of the different communions are part of the manifest body of Christ. To extend this metaphor, the manifest body of Christ, through schism, is in a state of Dissociative Identity Disorder or dissociation. So, in this Tenet, what we are recognizing is that all the different ecclesial communions have an aspect of the very stuff of the mind of Christ, however slanted or impure, and that when we draw on any or all of these in the therapeutic situation, it is not only good for our clients, but in some mysterious fashion, it's good for all of Christendom.

Doug: It is part of the healing of the manifest body of Christ.

Herman: I agree. I think we should somehow illustrate this truth ... because I can see people from almost any group objecting.

Julie: The whole is fragmented.

Doug: Into distinct parts.

Julie: Definitely!

Doug: And the parts miss each other desperately and do not know it. I

To concretize the diverse and valuable giftedness worked out in the various [Christian] communions, we could go on to talk about the healing value of the sacraments in Catholicism and Orthodoxy, the emphasis on revealed truth and ethical responsibility in evangelical Christianity, the importance of listening to God in Quakerism, and the efficacy of charismatic experience among Pentecostal denominations.

think it is a good analogy!

Charles: Right, well I think we see it clinically. Haven't you seen very hard-core bible-believing Protestant Christians longing for the sacrament of reconciliation or the Eucharist!

Doug: Right, then it is relegated to their shadow and erupts just when they have got it neatly suppressed.

Julie: And what wonderful creative energy comes from discovery of such suppressed spiritual hunger.

Doug: For example, I, and certain of my Protestant friends have been greatly blessed to "rediscover" the Catholic practice of praying for those who have died. To have a way to continue to love, through Jesus, those who have died has been very releasing and satisfying, like uncorking a stopped up flow of love and care.

6. Christian Holism *distinguishes itself as a psychological perspective in its conviction that men and women are made in the Image of God, therefore not only like God in nature and attributes, but made for relationship with God. It views images of humanity depicted in neuropsychology, psychoanalysis, cognitive-behaviorism, and phenomenological schools, etc. as useful but incomplete constructs of the human being. Drawing on scripture and theology,* Christian Holism *sees in the essential created human* Imago *a freedom to love, choose, create, and reason within the joy of an essential, lively, ebullient relation with God, self, others, and creation.* Christian Holism *finds that "made in the Image of God" implies a kinship between man and God and calls for the imitation of God as God is embodied in Jesus Christ.*

Charles: "Since [people are] made in God's Image every human being is worthy of honor and respect; [people are] neither to be murdered (Gen. 9:16) nor cursed (Jas. 3:9). 'Image' includes such characteristics as 'righteousness and holiness' (Eph. 4:24) and 'knowledge' (Col. 3:10). Believers are to be 'conformed to the likeness' of Christ (Rom. 8:29) and will someday be 'like him' (1 Jn. 3:2) [People are] the climax of God's creative activity, and God has 'crowned [human beings] with glory and honor'… (Ps. 8:5-8)" (NIV text note, 1985, p. 7).

Christian Holism appreciates that the reality of human nature lies within the Image of God (the *Imago Dei*) in people. Within the *Imago*, we find the reality of the individual person. The individual person is an entity like God, precious to God, worthy of honor—a creature to be well-treated and intrinsically lovable. *Christian Holism* acknowledges that the full glory of the person's humanity reflects the divinity of Christ.

Clinically, this means we draw upon models of human nature found in the various psychological schools and use them in service to the Spirit's work to repair and restore the true psychological substance of patients—that is, the Image of God in clients. But our therapy squarely faces the fact that final restoration of true human nature necessarily takes place as the result of God's supernatural, redemptive action alone—a restoration that is far beyond the reach of crude therapeutic technique or well-meaning theological or psychological babbling. In the end, therapist and client enjoy the truth that our deepest humanity is restored by God acting graciously.

In this particular Tenet, I am saying that we have a unique view of human nature that distinguishes itself from the other psychological doctrines, e.g. *Christian Holism*'s view of human nature is distinct from the reductive neuron doctrine of neuropsychology. We distinguish ourselves from the image of man as a talking beast or the aware animal of psychoanalysis. We go far beyond Cognitive Therapy and Rational-Emotive Therapy's image of man as a creature evolving into an ideal thinker and far beyond the radical behaviorists who see us as nothing more than a series of responses to stimuli. Our perspective of man is the *Imago Dei*—the likeness of the human creature to God.

Doug: This is one of the points I would tie back into the relational realm. The *Imago* is at the very core the ability to relate to God, in other words, the very capacity to be in union with God depends on this likeness. It is through this likeness that genuine relationship takes place. God created us to relate to God's self as grown up beings, beings with will, with intelligence, etc. So the very *Imago* nature of who we are reflects our being created for fellowship.

Robin: One of the first questions in the old Baltimore catechism (Gasparri, 1938, p. 1) was, "Why did God make you?" "God made me: to know Him, to love Him, and to serve Him in this world, so that I may be happy with Him in this life, and with him forever in heaven."

Charles: One of the things that I received from the Episcopal Catechism in *The Book of Common Prayer* (1977) about the *Imago* is "that we are free to make choices: to love, to create, to reason and to live in harmony with creation and with God" (p. 845). I would add *to live in harmony with oneself,* because I think that the whole Freudian image of man is as one containing inherent conflict among psychological structures. There is no inherent conflict within the human psyche in union with God because the *Imago* is restored.

Doug: We are intended for that perfect internal harmony. However, such inner harmony itself comes about in response to another, not in and of itself. So, we are not thinking of some perfect integration of a person. Actually, the person integrates in response to the other, most especially *the* Other and the others that are one's given community. It is in the engagement that this whole of holism occurs.

Charles: One of the things, too, that I think is so important is that Jesus of Nazareth fully incarnates the *Imago*. If you want to know who you are, who you really are, look at Jesus. He is fully man and fully God. He is the model, the role model if you will, and the reality and power of being fully human in union with God.

Doug: God gave us the model and relationship with the model and his powers.

7. The whole meaning of Imago, *at the root of everything, is homecoming. In other words, the whole pursuit of human life has to do with reconciliation, with God, with self, with those in the human community. We are meant to be in union with God, with others, within ourselves, with our generations, with nature. The goal of life is union or actually reunion. This is the beginning and ending, the whole thrust and meaning of healing. Wholeness grows from engagement of God and others and the natural world. And one's growing wholeness contributes to calling forth the wholeness of others, which develops as authentic response.*

Charles: Clients are brought home to themselves and rightly related to all things, because "the grace of God has triumphed in them" (McBrien, 1994, p. 1105). When the Spirit transforms people into themselves, the outcome is vast harmonization with all things that exist. This harmonization, this homecoming, is "a process, to be completed when the Kingdom of God is fully realized at the end of history ..." (McBrien, 1994, p. 1106). Treatment offers itself as a small part of this large process, becoming a vessel through which the Spirit pours its harmonizing grace, rightly ordering the patient's relationship with self, God, others, history, and creation. Through this grace the client—after being blessed to face the problems of human pain—is exited from disorder and brought home to all good things. This homecoming is Spirit-driven, dynamic, and ongoing.

Doug: Holism concerns more than my interior wholeness. My true wholeness actually has to do with union with God, with others, with creation. In other words, to be whole is to be reunited. Now, in that reuniting, I am reunited within myself as well. That is part of the incarnation of it. And I must gather myself in order to make a whole response to others.

Holism concerns more than my interior wholeness. My true wholeness actually has to do with union with God, with others, with creation. In other words, to be whole is to be reunited. Now, in that reuniting, I am reunited within myself as well. That is part of the incarnation of it. And I must gather myself in order to make a whole response to others.

Charles: One of the things that this whole dialogue is pulling out of me is how relational thinking is such a part of *Christian Holism*. One of the things that seems to be Doug's specialty is to keep bringing out the idea that this is not an just an abstract thing involving Platonic idealism and static, perfected states. Becoming whole involves an ongoing dynamic relationship.

Julie: The process has to include specific embodiment.

Doug: Right, exactly, because God's power is exercised in love, and for restoration. Love would not restore somebody to something they are not. And restoration includes restoration of relationships as they are intended to be, which means all levels. So performing miracles—which has its place— must be for what God intends in the recreation of the human order between us, specifically and particularly. That is what I meant by Holism. The action is always in the context of the whole. The whole person is always the whole relatedness of the whole person ... cell to cell ...

Charles: ...person to person ...

Doug: ... person to legacy, person to whole body of Jesus, person to friendship ... God never has less than every item of the whole in mind, spe- cifically.

Charles: Let me add in here how we relate to pain in the context of Ho- lism. *Christian Holism* does not have a naïve approach to pain. Pain is a part of the whole picture of the unfolding divinization of humanity in relation- ship. Pain is an indicator that something is not right. We listen to pain to hear what it is speaking, what it means. Letting pain speak is part of the healing process, part of being made whole. Pain is an indicator that can guide us home to whole relationship.

Julie: And the Holy Spirit enters into the depths of all our pain ... with- out reservation. Jesus made the way for this by experiencing the extremes of human pain, knowing human pain completely as a human being.

Doug: And our capacity to be present to our own pain ... actually be pre- sent to our own pain ... completely, depends on the presence of the Holy Spirit. There is no capacity without the presence of the Holy Spirit.

Charles: Can you say more about that?

Doug: Yes, you cannot sustain presence to your own pain and know its meaning without the presence of the Holy Spirit to undergird you, and to manifest your pain to you in its accurate terms. Also, the Holy Spirit completely identifies with you, so you are not alone with your pain. Whether one recognizes this consciously or not, I believe that the reality of the Holy Spirit's presence makes pain bearable. With the Holy Spirit's presence one can sustain presence to one's own pain and presence to someone else's pain, without having to close it off, without having to objectify it, without having to exclude one's self from it, or deny one's responsibility in it or defend any other awareness which is necessary for reconciliation/healing.

8. Christian Holism *offers a specific view of psychological treatment and healing. It submits treatment to the Divine's intention for complete redemption of people, to reverse the damaging impact of the Fall, to end levels and sources of separation from God, and to conclude alienation from the* Imago Dei. *This is done by placing social science under the Lordship of Jesus Christ. Under Christ's dominion, treatment relies on natural therapeutic processes and supernatural grace to accomplish these healings.*

Christian Holism *finds that natural therapeutic processes are available through psychotherapy and the application of medicines.* Christian Holism *finds that the benefits of natural therapeutic processes unfold over time.*

Christian Holism *also appreciates the reality of supernatural grace. Supernatural grace comes directly to the beloved as the result of God's sovereign activity on the beloved's behalf. The benefits of supernatural grace can be instantaneous.*

Charles: The purpose of treatment includes but exceeds the mitigation of clinical syndromes and character pathology. With God's help, treatment becomes a part of the unfolding of God's profoundly healing purpose for the client. This involves remission of personal and inherited sins through the work and person of Jesus Christ, restoration of communion with God, and restoration of harmonious communion with self and others. *Christian Holism* annexes social science into the Kingdom of God, and the Holy Spirit is asked to enter the clinical situation. Then either of two forms of healing may occur: a) healing that occurs through evident natural means, or b) healing that occurs through evident supernatural means.

It may please God, for example, to allow people to get well through good things in the created order like antidepressants or cognitive restructuring. Or it may please God to heal a mood disorder immediately, directly, and supernaturally. Because *Christian Holism* finds the Holy Spirit to be clinically present and supremely competent, it finds natural therapeutic processes and supernatural healing both to contain equal measures of God's grace.

Doug: We should work with this notion of transcending natural processes, because remarkable healing may be the presence of a higher order principle or way of relating under which the "natural process" or development is actually subsumed and transformed, just like Jesus says, "I came not to abolish the Law, but to fulfill the Law." Yet in one sense by fulfilling the law, by fulfilling the law of love, he in a sense dissolved some of the minor laws, at least the way minor laws were understood or applied.

Charles: So there's higher law.

Doug: There may be a transcending way of relating that God engages with us which subsumes "natural" development and seems to set it aside and yet, if we could see its operations, we would understand how the "miraculous" includes the "natural." For example, with the new theory of Physics suddenly the old ways of understanding seem to pass away, but actually previous theory is subsumed into a transformed way of seeing and understanding. These transcending ways could be like, in Sheldrake's (1988) terms, lower order "laws of nature" from a perspective of field theory can be seen as the operation of habits that actually are not fixed or unchangeable, but only change ever so gradually over time. It is just that they seem to operate with certain regularities that appear and reappear but that does not mean that they are not changing.

Robin: When I wrote a review (Caccese, 1994) of Larry Dossey's first book on Prayer (1993), I struggled to communicate the concepts of the new Physics on which Dossey was basing his thesis of the effectiveness of prayer. The only way I could help people and myself to try to grasp what the new Physics does with ways we are used to looking at our reality was to say, "This isn't Kansas anymore." This did not mean that "Kansas" no longer existed. Some concepts, such as the notions of cause and effect or of linear time, as we are used to thinking of them, no longer apply in all circumstances. So, there was a way in which I needed to transcend my old ways of thinking … transcend, but not abandon. I do not think the new Physics would say, for example, that the notion of linear time does not exist or is not valid, but that there is more to the notion of time than just thinking of time as linear. Similarly, cause and effect are valid ways of looking at our reality, but now there is also the valid notion of Chaos Theory. Our world becomes a both/and world in lots of ways.

Julie: I am just thinking about how I image this spectrum from grace through nature to miraculous healing. When there is a block to the Lord's grace, at times the Lord will just remove that block, come in and sovereignly remove obstacles. At other times there is something to be learned, something for the person to work at. We have our part, our human part, as client and therapist. We have what we have discovered, our body of knowledge that is to be exercised.

Robin: That makes me think of blood clots. There are certain drugs that can just kind of go "blast" to a blood clot to dissolve it, but in other circumstances it is better to administer smaller doses of heparin or coumadin to gradually dissolve the clot. This slower dissolving process seems similar to the process of learning something in the midst of the healing process.

Doug: At times God blasts through. Jesus reaches in and touches the wound. At other times, the person has to do some of the work themselves. Jesus is not going to do it all. The person is being called to be Jesus to themselves. They are ready. They have to be Jesus to themselves. The Lord's role is going to be there coaching.

Julie: That's right. At those times the person has to engage themselves, be responsible for being a healing presence to themselves, apprehend the grace they have been given and apply it in their own inner world, as you say, with Jesus coaching. However, sometimes no matter what you do as a therapist, the person will not choose to be responsible in his or her own healing.

Doug: Then you have to just wait or go around another way. For some reason the person is not ready or willing to choose the way being offered.

Charles: God respects choice.

Doug: So, I suppose, God respects resistance.

Charles: Say that again.

Doug: Like in any good therapy, we respect resistance.

Robin: Gestalt methodology does that.

Doug: Yes and personifies it and works with it as a voice. Most psychotherapeutic methodologies respect resistance. Often resistance is a bad image of the outcome, like self-responsibility will mean abandonment. Respecting resistance gets back to the *Imago*. We are created with will and are to grow in choosing. Resistance can be seen as a "no," an implicit choice, therefore to be respected and investigated.

Charles: So, we have decided that God heals in terms of therapeutic process and miraculously and that the interplay of grace and free will will determine treatment courses and outcomes.

9. Christian Holism employs both "secular" (psychological and relational-ethical) and "sacred" (spiritual-biblical) interventions to participate in the Holy Spirit's ministry to the client. Christian Holism employs tools like psychodynamic insight, cognitive restructuring, dream work, and other interventions along with healing of memories, forgiveness, confession, and other spiritually based therapies.

Charles: Simply put, it is the experience of practitioners of *Christian Holism* that God utilizes both secular and sacred therapies to achieve wholeness in patients. For this reason, the resources of social science are viewed as holy and the accouterments of faith are seen as therapeutic.

In terms of interventions that we utilize in *Christian Holism*, what healing modalities do we engage on behalf of our clients?

Doug: First I prepare myself, then I prepare the place, and I tend my own healing and spiritual nurture before the person arrives. Of course, I am always in the process of my own healing work.

This idea of being aware of one's own woundedness, to remain humble and open to the client in this way is good, because it maintains the therapist in a servant role, being available to provide compassion and to identify with the human struggle of the person.

Charles: What else?

Doug: Part of my preparation is to sense my own vulnerabilities with the particular person and to take care of myself as I enter into a session with the person. I will sometimes do an assessment of my response to the person, particularly if I am not looking forward to that person coming in for a session. I try to get in touch with my anxieties. Then I attempt to identify, as best I can, what they are about and take care of them in the sense of at least putting them in a safe place where they will be tended. For example, I put them in Jesus' heart or put them in an interior place within an attitude of caring for myself, of compassion for myself, so I know I have accounted for my anxieties as best I can in a self-loving way. Then I use my emotions and felt states, as I anticipate the person's presence, also as potentially informing me about the person as well. These not only alerting me as to what is going to be triggered in me, but also alert me to what the trigger in me reveals about the person and about what is happening between us.

Julie: As I look at my own brokenness and where I am stuck, I gain a compassion and patience for the client in their stuckness, so that I am not so annoyed when they are slow to change.

Charles: In psychodynamic terms this is about countertransferential issues. But there is a real humanity here that goes beyond mere countertransference. This idea of being aware of one's own woundedness, to remain humble and open to the client in this way is good, because it maintains the therapist in a servant role, being available to provide compassion and to identify with the human struggle of the person.

Julie: Even from the perspective of psychoanalytic ethics, one would be expected to carry his or her own shadow or vulnerabilities or whatever, especially if you are going to ask the client to face their own dark side and especially to protect the client from one's own projections.

Doug: Yes, from trying to fix oneself in one's client, and then acting out one's own frustration with oneself on the client.

Charles: I was not expecting the discussion to go this way. I thought everyone was going to jump in to talk about healing prayer, dream work, etc., but it sounds as though part of our Holism clearly involves the person of the therapist being conscious of self and tending to self as well as the spiritual environs that the client will be entering.

Doug: Therapists need to tend to themselves in the same way that they

The power or release techniques such as EMDR, Thought Field Therapy, Neuro-Emotional Technique, etc. actually integrate very easily with healing of memories prayers. In fact, I am finding EMDR very helpful in the context of healing prayer particularly when the person is not able to use effectively explicit imagery of Jesus.

are going to be teaching the client to do.

Charles: What about treatment methods and techniques?

Doug: Well, I tend to think abstractly, so I have kind of divided the territory up. My techniques are going to focus on the person's relationship with themselves, with others, family, etc., with legacy and with God. So then my techniques come under these focuses. Sometimes I am dealing with all of these relationships at the same time, sometimes sequentially. For example, healing of memories prayers and imagery may focus in on a person's relationship to self first and then out toward healing relationships with the others' who were participants in the particular memories that are being treated. Then, as relationships are addressed, the focus may shift to generations, to those ancestors whose lives have been of consequence for the painful situation being remembered.

I put Cognitive Therapy in the category of the person relating to self. The person becomes conscious of their own cognitions, conscious of their belief systems, and the therapist is helping them imagine options and make choices to dismantle certain cognitions and construct other ones. In that context, you also realize there are emotional charges involved and sometimes there are other kinds of healing modalities that are needed to undergird or even free the cognitive changes to be able to happen, such as the healing of memories in which the beliefs originated or the releasing of stuck emotional patterns through using EMDR (Eye Movement Desensitization and Reprocessing) or another techniques of release.

Charles: Go into those.

Doug: The release techniques?

Charles: Yes.

Doug: The power or release techniques such as EMDR, Thought Field Therapy, Neuro-Emotional Technique, etc. actually integrate very easily with healing of memories prayers. In fact, I am finding EMDR very helpful in the context of healing prayer particularly when the person is not able to use effectively explicit imagery of Jesus. In some cases imagining Jesus is too problematic in the person's inner theology. Their negative projections onto God are too powerful to access any imagery of divine persons for the sake of healing. No matter what we do, the person's image of Jesus, if they can or are willing to image Jesus at all, is always a false Jesus, judgmental, condemning, very much appearing like one of the person's parents as the person has described their experience of that parent. So, I say, forget it. Do EMDR and pray, asking God to heal without any explicit theological imagery. Then proceed, watch, wait, and be alert for how the Holy Spirit's activity is going to manifest.

Charles: You are basically affirming to the person that God is acting for their benefit through interventions.

Robin: The more the therapist does this and accumulates experience with manifestations of the Holy Spirit's activity, a backlog of experiences develops which enhances the therapist's confidence in God's presence and faithfulness in all interventions.

Doug: One thing that I use often, especially inwardly in my own imagination, is imagery of Jesus with the person. This is part of a prayer. I am asking Jesus to show me how he is relating to this person. Then I tune into my inner imagery of Jesus, watch his actions, hear his words, feel the quality of his relating to the person. Then I try to incorporate my sense of Jesus' way with the person into my approach to the person. So I try to manifest the way in which I am discerning that Jesus is relating to the person into my responding to that person.

Charles: What is your process of manifesting to the client such an inner experience of Jesus?

Doug: I pray and ask the Holy Spirit for an impression of Jesus' approach to this person and sometimes I will actually voice Jesus words or attitude, as I sense him, to the "child" within the person. Sometimes I will simply take on the attitude I sense, the manner, not so much as an actor, but let it infuse me so that I am approaching the person in that spirit. Sometimes I speak more tentatively as in, "is it alright with you if I tell you what I think I hear Jesus saying to you?" At times, persons need a lot of help in the healing of memories. They are too wounded to imagine anything positive, but if I say, "You know what I see Jesus doing, what I hear him saying?" and then begin to share what I see or hear, all I have to do is it get a sentence into it and they say, "Oh yeah, I see him, I see him now." Then they will pick up and continue or then they will get started but quickly run dry because they are so wounded. Then I will say, "Well, you know ...," and they pick up again, "Now I see, OK, he is picking me up now." That is sort of how it goes.

Julie: What you are saying is that you are using spiritual gifts.

Robin: I had an experience like this when I prayed with a woman. This woman had had a very negative dream. I tried asking her where Jesus was in the dream and she was getting nothing. In the dream, she was sitting in the passenger seat of a car and the other person driving the car had just done something terribly crude. She just could not see Jesus or imagine Jesus in that dream. I prayed longer in silence, but I finally said, "You know, I think Jesus is leaning right on the window next to you, looking at you and saying, 'Pretty crude, huh'?" She broke out laughing and began seeing Jesus very graphically.

Charles: Let's move the discussion. I want to highlight that secular paradigms and therapy interventions are actively used by the Holy Spirit. The Spirit can use secular interventions as effectively as "spiritual."

Julie: In terms of interventions, the Holy Spirit is truth, shining through, revealing and leading, through whatever method or technique we are using. We can never put the Spirit in a conceptual box and say this is how the Holy Spirit works. This is the method that is truly of the Spirit.

Charles: So we are annexing conceptually all this truthful secular material right into the Kingdom of God and putting it in service to our work.

Julie: Well, we want to see where truth is.

Robin: What I see in our dialogue, is that in this process we are being released from the tyranny of definitions and methodologies, in both secular-professional and spiritual-theological worlds, released from the tyranny of being held tightly to specific definitions and methodologies.

Doug: God reveals God's self and God's ways in that secular piece of knowledge and technique. God reveals within the created order and helps us to discover how the created order works in the human personality. We are not annexing something into therapy that is alien to God. We annex that within creation that reveals the nature of God and the nature of God's creation. It is not an integration in the sense of trying to fit everything together. It is seeing the truth revealed—whatever it is—whether it is a piece of psychoanalytic theory or Jungian theory or Contextual Theory, whatever. It may get remapped and reshaped as we allow Jesus to work it into our schema, but there is truth there, truth that heals.

Herman: All truth is God's truth and my responsibility is to bring it under the dominion of Christ.

Robin: Again, the bottom line is "If you abide in my word, you shall be my disciples indeed, and you shall know the truth …

Doug: … and the truth shall set you free" (John 8:32).

10. Christian Holism *is practiced by a therapist who provides sanctuary in which the client's healing process can unfold. The therapist does this by attending to his or her own psycho-spiritual issues, withholding judgment in humility, borrowing the Holy Spirit's therapeutic love of the client, and honing psychotherapeutic expertise, all as a fellow traveler, a brother or sister in the body of Jesus, in the Body of God.*

Charles: The therapist's intention is to offer the client a safe clinical environment in which to heal, a sanctuary. In this sanctuary, the therapist further does not hide behind professional vanity. Understanding himself or her-

... in this process we are being released from the tyranny of definitions and methodologies, in both secular-professional and spiritual-theological worlds, released from the tyranny of being held tightly to specific definitions and methodologies.

self to be in need of grace, the therapist provides service to the client in humility. To the extent possible, the therapist will have such good will for the client that he or she will embody the Spirit's love for the client. This is understood to be a charism to be well-guarded against inappropriateness—but essential to the healing process. Further, practitioners of *Christian Holism* develop clinical expertise, recognizing that the Spirit enhances naturally obtained clinical skills by supernaturally empowering them in service to the therapy of brother and sister clients.

Doug: The therapist is always a brother or sister of the client in the body of Jesus even though the roles are maintained for the sake of healing. The therapist carries a consciousness and the reality that we are all children, siblings of the Father.

Julie: Also, the therapist is often a litter bearer.

Robin: Like the people who brought the paralyzed man to Jesus in Luke 5: 17-26. The therapist is also like a midwife.

Charles: As a litter bearer, the therapist brings the client to Christ.

Doug: The therapist helps to create a way to Jesus.

Robin: And, as a midwife, the therapist assists in the birthing process.

Julie: Facilitates birthing.

Charles: ... the ongoing process of being born again.

Doug: ... in the sense of the ongoing birth and rebirth of all facets of the person. We are not talking about just the primary experience of being born again but of *ongoing* healing and birthing and development of facets of the person.

Herman: The new birth is a mysterious, momentary experience, but conversion is a lifetime process.

Charles: ... from current woundedness to true person.

Julie: ... from image to likeness. Sometimes the therapist is a person who offers a holding environment, a womb. The therapist gives the person a place to be safe, a contained space, or a container.

Doug: We offer a holding environment and even a sanctuary. Sanctuary is a safe place psychologically and spiritually. For us, this includes the prayer preparation and the spiritual preparation of the office as well as the manner of responding to the person.

Julie: Biblically, a sanctuary was a holy place ... where a fugitive was safe from arrest or violence, a place where the person's life was held sacred.

Doug: In the old days, a sanctuary made you safe from the law.

Charles: The practitioner of *Christian Holism* provides a place to make people safe from the law, even safe from the law that they carry within them (as in the superego). The superego can act like an internal cop that will not allow them to discuss their reality or allow their ego to offer the necessary part of themselves to the Holy Spirit for dialogue and healing.

Doug: When we provide a sanctuary, we refuse to prejudge anything or anyone. We just create a space where the person is free from attack, not judged, and helped to release themselves from their own condemnations and prejudgments.

Julie: The therapy is the window to the holy sanctuary of God. The therapist can be a channel.

Charles: The therapist is a person who operates on behalf of the client with the understanding that, regardless of the degree of psychological disturbance or conflict, the Holy Spirit is operating on behalf of your client. The therapist wants to be part of that.

Doug: ... and is present with the full love of God, period, even when the therapist cannot understand how Love is going to operate and cannot see it. I cannot say I always see it, but I maintain the conviction that it always operates.

Julie: In some ways then, the faith of the therapist *carries* the person for that moment.

Doug: Right, that is like the *litter*, the illustration of the litter, because the person on the litter is not able to bring themselves.

Julie: So the other people bring them to Christ.

Doug: Your faith brings them.

Robin: If you put that in the imagery of a labor coach, it is like that person is in labor and the reasoning process that you were going through is like coaching the breathing, breathing with faith.

Doug: Now the thing you actually cannot do as the labor coach is the pushing.

Julie: That is where the person has to have their own will.

Doug: Yes, because the role of the person's will is crucial. Sometimes you have to back up and back up and back up to find it. Sometimes the only will I can engage with the person is their willingness to let me pray. They are willing to join me in the sense of endorsing the use of my faith on their behalf. Sometimes that is all I have. But it is enough.

Conclusion

As an approach to mental health treatment, *Christian Holism* is comprised of several important tenets. Among these foundational principles is the Central Tenet: the assertion that the Holy Spirit is fully present and active in the clinical situation. Other important tenets of *Christian Holism* are as follows: Treatment is conducted under the Lordship of Jesus Christ. Psychological theories and interventions are annexed into the kingdom of God by placing them at the disposal of the Holy Spirit. Under the Spirit's guidance, scripture inspires and guides psychotherapeutic practice. Creeds and catechisms open clinicians and clients to the healing reality of God. Ecumenical in outlook and practice, treatment welcomes and loves all the healing gifts contained within Christendom. Conceptualized in terms of the Image of God (*Imago Dei*), essential human nature implies a freedom to love, choose, create, and reason within the joy of a lively ebullient relation with God, self, others, and creation. Treatment participates in the reunion of the person with all good things, including God, self, others, and creation. Natural healing processes and miraculous healing are recognized as having equal measures of God's grace; both are excellent and equally welcome in the healing process. *Christian Holism* finds that, under grace, social science is holy and faith is therapeutic. Practitioners of this therapy view themselves as fellow travelers with clients and humbly participate in God's healing love for the client.

These tenets are not meant to be exhaustive or unchangeable. Rather, they are meant to guide the use of this transpersonal psychological theory and practice in the context of the Christian clinical situation. As the Holy Spirit continues to unfold God's plan, the tenets of *Christian Holism* will expand and change. This must necessarily happen, because the tenets of Christian Holism are subject to the love and pleasure of a Living God.

References

The amplified bible. (1987). Grand Rapids, MI: Zondervan Publishing House.

Barker, K. (Ed.). (1985). *The NIV study bible*. Grand Rapids, MI: Zondervan Bible Publishers.

Caccese, R. (1994). Healing prayer in era III medicine. *The Journal of Christian Healing, 16(1)*: 38-41.

Dossey, L (1993). *Healing words: The power of prayer and the practice of medicine*. San Francisco, CA: Harper.

Fabricant, S. and Schoeninger, D. (1987). Evaluating methods and theories of healing. *The Journal of Christian Healing, 9(1)*: 35-41.

Gasparri, P. Cardinal (1938). *Catholic faith based on the catholic catechism*. (Felix M. Kirsch, O.F.M.C.A.P., Ph.D., Litt.D. and Sister M. Brendan, I.H.M, M.A. (Ed.s), book three of a series. Washington, DC: The Catholic University of America Press.

Guilbert, C. (Custodian). (1977). *The book of common prayer*. New York: The Church Hymnal Corporation and The Seabury Press.

McBrien, R. (1994). *Catholicism*. New York: HarperCollins.

Peterson, E. (1995). *The message*. Colorado Springs, CO: Navpress.

Sears, R. (1999). A Christian approach to discerning spiritualities. *The Journal of Christian Healing, 21(1):*15-34.

Sheldrake, R. (1988). *The presence of the past*. New York: Random House.

United States Catholic Conference, (1994). *Catechism of the catholic church*. New York: Doubleday.

Douglas Schoeninger, Ph.D. is President of the Institute for Christian Counseling and Therapy in West Chester, PA and former editor of the Journal of Christian Healing. *Doug maintains a private psychotherapy practice rooted in prayer, specifically focused on the healing of families. Doug has a Ph.D. from the University of Wisconsin where he studied with Carl Rogers, Ph.D. Doug has also studied Contextural Family Therapy with Ivan Nagy, M.D. and Barbara Krasner, Ph.D. and has trained in applied kinesiology and neuroemotional techniques with Scott Walker, D.C. and Theresa Dale, Ph.D., N.D. He collaborated extensively with Kenneth McAll, M.D. in the area of healing the family tree.*

Rev. Herman Riffel was born in a Mennonite family in Saskatchewan, Canada, but the family soon moved to California. Feeling called to the ministry he studied at Multnomah School of the Bible in Portland, OR, at Wheaton College in Wheaton, IL and at the C.G. Jung Institute for Analytical Psychology in Zurich, Switzerland. He served as a Baptist pastor in Michigan and Illinois for twenty five years. As God opened his life to the Holy Spirit he also opened the door for Herman to minister to missionaries around the world, and to be invited to give eight hours of lectures to priests and nuns at the Vatican in Rome and to lecture to the Jung Society of Sydney, Australia. This resulted in requests for his material and the writing of the books: Christian Maturity and the Spirit's Power, The Voice of God, Learning to Recognize God's Voice, Dreams: Wisdom Within, Dream Interpretation: A Biblical Understanding *and* Dreams: Giants and Geniuses in the Making.

Robin Caccese, B.S., M.T.(A.S.C.P.), trained as a Medical Technologist after receiving her BS degree in biology from Albright College in 1971. She worked for eighteen years as a research assistant in the Department of Pharmacology at Temple Medical School in Philadelphia. She began working part-time for the Journal of Christian Healing *in 1985 when the* Journal *was in need of a person with computer skills. When her job in research ended in 1990, Robin became the* Journal's *Managing Editor and has continued to expand her commitment to the* Journal *with her editorial skills as well as her skills in computer typesetting and layout. Robin has a passion to understand and articulate the nature of healing, especially the integration of medical/scientific healing modalities with Christian healing modalities. Robin also has a deep heart for persons recovering from incest and child sexual abuse.*

Julie Wegryn, MS, MAT, NCC is a Licensed Psychologist, a Licensed Professional Counselor, and a National Certified Counselor. She obtained degrees from Douglas College of Rutgers University and The College of New Jersey. Julie is a certified teacher who instructed in the area of Special Education and Vocational Rehabilitation of multiply handicapped persons for 17 years. During this time she obtained a degree in Counseling and Human Relations from Villanova University and completed the requirements to become a psychotherapist. She obtained training in healing prayer from Elijah House Ministry and as part of her ongoing training and her many years practicing at the Institute for Christian Counseling and Therapy. Julie has been in private practice for many years in New Jersey and Pennsylvania. She specializes in integrating healing prayer, counseling and Christian Spirituality guided by the Holy Spirit and Biblical principles. Julie's areas of interest include depth psychology, spiritual and emotional healing, and relationship issues for individuals and couples.

A Christian Depth Psychology Of Forgiveness Leading to *the Resurrection Effect**

Charles L. Zeiders, Psy.D.

Forgiveness may be the key to healing deep psychological wounds. This article develops a Christian depth psychology of forgiveness, employing psychological theory as an exegetical tool for developing the teachings of Jesus of Nazareth in Matthew 5:22-26 into a theory of how *Core Wounds* become imprisoned within the psyche. This article offers a psychotherapeutic prayer protocol for healing wounded core areas of the psyche based on that same scripture. This article places the forgiveness intervention in the context of social science, orthodox Christian theology, and addresses the Holy Spirit's presence in the treatment situation. Clinical examples of what the author calls *the Resurrection Effect,* a natural outcome of effective forgiveness, are provided in case studies.

W hen Jesus of Nazareth answered St. Peter's question, "Lord, how often must I forgive my brother if he wrongs me? Seven times?", Peter was undoubtedly astonished to hear his Master's reply, "Not seven, I tell you, but seventy seven times" (Matt. 18:21-22, NJB). Like us, Peter lived in an age of retribution. Why did the Son of Man insist on this departure from conventional wisdom? Why advise such radical forgiveness? In part, the answer lies in Jesus' advanced knowledge of human nature. Knowing both the mind of God and the mind of man, Jesus understood that human nature resembles divine nature. Jesus commanded forgiveness, because he knew that unforgiveness imprisons us in a *Will to Punish* that locks us into our woundedness. He knew that the *Will to Forgive* culminates in a mental posture that frees us from the prison of the woundedness that others origi-

* This article is an editorial reworking of the author's three articles on forgiveness. #1. "A Christian Depth Psychology of Forgiveness Leading to the Resurrection Effect," *The Journal of Christian Healing*, Volume 21, #2, Summer, 1999, pp. 3-23; #2. "Forgiveness, Christian Holism and the Resurrection Effect," *The Journal of Christian Healing*, Volume 22, #3&4, Fall/Winter, 2001, pp 42-57 and #3. "Forgiveness and Healing the Repetition Compulsion," Charles Zeiders, Psy.D. & Julie Wegryn, M.A., *A Primer for Christian Healthcare Practice*, (2001), The Association of Christian Therapists: McLean, VA, pp. 155-164.

nally inflict upon us. The *Will to Forgive* opens the way to our healing.

As a Christian clinical psychologist, trained in Cognitive Therapy and versed in depth psychology, I am impressed by Our Lord's teachings about forgiveness. Today, as in the first century, Jesus' position was, and remains, counter-intuitive. Given the current state of human nature, the *Will to Punish* remains the most native of our responses to those who wrong us. And the *Will to Punish* feels most authentic to us. But depth analysis of Jesus' teaching shows that what appears right and feels right is actually wrong. From a psychological point of view, the *Will to Punish* harms us. What I hope to demonstrate is that Jesus' teachings on forgiveness provide a template for healing psychological woundedness, that His teachings make scientific, theological, and clinical sense for those seeking to restore the Image of God in themselves and mankind. Most importantly, I hope to demonstrate the clinical usefulness of praying according to the healing protocol implicit in Jesus' teaching in Matthew 5:23-24 and Mark 11:25. I believe Jesus' teachings on forgiveness contain depth psychological insight about how we might pray to successfully heal even profound psychological woundedness. The health efficacy of Christ's forgiveness message, in particular, and the Christian revelation, in general, is scientifically supported.

What is Forgiveness?

In theorizing and researching the phenomenon, forgiveness experts have developed various definitions of forgiveness. Aponte's and Enright's are among them. Aponte (1998) proposes that:

> ... forgiveness at its core is a freely made intention to let go of the bitter debt to which we hold another. It is a desire to let go that grows out of a commitment to free oneself and the other person from the bondage of debt and hurt, however grievous (p. 41).

Freedman and Enright (1996) propose that interpersonal forgiveness is defined as:

> ... an unjustly hurt person's act of deliberately giving up resentment toward an offender while fostering the undeserved qualities of beneficence and compassion toward the offender. Forgiveness is in the context of deep injustice in contrast to every day annoyance. There is a decidedly paradoxical quality to forgiveness as the forgiver gives up the resentment to which he has a right and gives the gift of compassion to which the offender has no right (p. 983).

The definition of forgiveness that I use clinically to guide my treatment interventions with Christian patients is:

Jesus commanded forgiveness, because he knew that unforgiveness imprisons us in a *Will to Punish* that locks us into our woundedness.

the intentional replacement of the *Will to Punish* those who harm with the *Will to Forgive*. Forgiveness is an exercise of free will, conducted before the face of God, with the formal intention to abandon the pursuit of equal harm to the harmer. Forgiveness is grounded fully in the ego of the forgiver and results in healing psychological complexes outside the ego's control through the power of the Holy Spirit in the name of Jesus Christ.

While all three definitions of forgiveness are adequate, high-lighting the re-linquishment of a retributive stance toward an offender for the purpose of psychological healing, my definition puts God in the object-relations mix, landing the definition within the emerging theistic therapeutic paradigm (Zeiders and Schaller, 1998) and the Judeo-Christian tradition. To my mind, God must be included in the definition of forgiveness, because the Holy Spirit responds in a mind-restoring way to the *Will to Forgive*. I will develop this idea after a quick look at some scientific research into forgiveness.

Scientific Research on Forgiveness

Scientific evidence exists that forgiveness, both within and without a the-istic context, correlates with psychological healing. One study of special value was conducted by Freedman and Enright (1996). Although small in sample size, their outcome results on the effects of forgiveness upon female incest survivors were provocative. The study involved 12 female incest sur-vivors randomly divided into a forgiveness treatment group and a wait-list control group. The treatment group attended weekly individual psychother-apy sessions over the course of a year, during which time they received a standardized 17 point forgiveness protocol. At the conclusion of treatment, the forgiveness group had gained more than the control group in forgiving their victimizers and they experienced increased hope. Moreover, their de-pression and anxiety scores fell below that of the no treatment control group, raising the possibility that there is a relationship between forgiveness and peace and happiness. When the control group participated in the forgiveness intervention, it made similar gains as the original treatment group. Examina-tion of individual cases showed that forgivers were able to emotionally heal as they relinquished resentment of their perpetrators. Some participants were even able to reconcile with them. Importantly, the forgiveness intervention correlates to what appears to be a healing of both emotional states and healthy object-relations ability.

Other scientific research on forgiveness shows similar hopeful findings:

1. Al-Mabuk, Enright, Cardis (1995), in a study among adolescent children who felt inadequately loved by their parents, demonstrated that the children experienced decreased anxiety and depression and increased self-esteem following forgiveness interventions. They were taught how to forgive—and after they forgave their parents, they felt better about themselves.

2. Coyle and Enright, (1997) showed that men hurt by their female partner's decision to have an abortion experienced decreased anger, anxiety, and grief following a forgiveness intervention targeted to foster forgiveness for the person they blamed most for the abortion.

3. Hebl and Enright, (1993) found that among 24 elderly Christian females who struggled with a forgiveness issue, those in the treatment group who scored higher on forgiveness demonstrated increased self-esteem and lower anxiety and depression levels than those in the non-forgiveness group.

4. A cross sectional study of over 1,000 adults during a 1988 poll statistically established that negative life satisfaction relates to resentment of offenders and positive life satisfaction relates to praying for people who hurt us. So, in this Gallup poll, forgivers appear more satisfied with their lives than resentful non-forgivers (Poloma and Gallop, 1988) .

5. Among outcomes measured in a study by Dr. Robert Enright [1] validating the Enright Forgiveness Inventory—a 60 item forgiveness scale that assesses positive and negative aspects of behavior, cognition, and affect toward an offending person—anxiety levels decreased as forgiveness scores increased (Subkoviak, Enright, Wu, Gassin, Freedman, Olson, and Sarinopoulos, 1995).

6. van Oyen Witvliet, C., Ludwig, T., and Vander Laan, K. (2001) in a fascinating study attempted to measure the physiological responses of forgiveness. In their study, 36 men and 35 women, who were connected to biofeedback equipment, were asked to think of someone who hurt them and to think about all the things that they would like to do to punish those people. The biofeedback equipment registered dramatic physiological changes—from increased muscle tension to heart rate. As the participants thought about hurting the people who trespassed against them, their own bodies were ravaged. When they were told to think of forgiving the people who had hurt them, something different happened: their bodies quieted into normal ranges. The conclusion of these researchers was that forgiving people is probably good, not only for your emotional health, but also physical health. The researchers believe that further research is likely to show that forgivers will have fewer coronary problems.

Forgiveness Myths

Before I further define true forgiveness, I would like to explore what forgiveness is not. I have drawn these ideas from Caine and Kaufman (1999, p. 285) and developed them.

1. Forgiveness is not sanctioning and condoning abusive behavior. True forgiveness recognizes that something wrong occurred.
2. Forgiveness is not conditional. We do not say: "I'll forgive you if you change." Forgiveness is predicated on an act of the will. We say: "I forgive the person who trespasses against me regardless of whether or not they repent."
3. Forgiveness is not reconciliation. It is a separate construct from reconciliation. Many people who forgive should create huge boundaries between themselves and the people who have trespassed against them.
4. Forgiveness is not denial. If someone is too quick to forgive, and their anger is not available to their ego, they are probably in denial. My recommendation is to not pursue forgiveness until the person doing the forgiving is in touch with their anger.
5. Forgiveness is not forgetting. We do not want to forget legitimate learning about fallen human nature. If somebody hurts you, and you forgive them, maintain a wide boundary between yourself and them. Do not assume that your forgiveness has changed the person who hurt you. Forgiveness is the forgiver's project, not the trespasser's. One's forgiveness does not necessarily heal or influence the other person. Human nature is fallen, and people are capable of sadism, abuse, and grotesque behaviors that will again hurt us. Jesus knows this truth. In Matthew 10:17 Jesus warns, "Be on your guard against men." Our Lord's words are important for the forgiveness enterprise. We forgive, but we do not pretend that the people we have forgiven have been touched by God or that reconciliation is possible. Even though we forgive in this life, we might have to wait for the next life to enjoy full community with those who have harmed us.

What is True Forgiveness? How Does Psychological Healing Work?

1. Forgiveness is acknowledging that a person has wounded you by trespassing against you.
2. Forgiveness is acknowledging a *Will to Punish* the offending person. The client becomes aware of an intention to hurt their offender in a manner that will balance the damage the offender inflicted on them. The client, for example, may calculate, "This person inflicted six units of pain on me; I will inflict six units of pain on them." That is the *Will to Punish*.
3. Through an act of *Will* before God in prayer, the forgiver asserts a *Will*

> **Research studies support the notion that forgiveness can contribute powerfully to psychological healing and well-being. Science may well establish that forgiveness consistently produces a healing, restorative effect on a variety of outcome measures.**

to Forgive the trespasser over and above their *Will to Punish* the trespasser.

4. Forgiveness is a change of mind—not a change of heart. In this forgiveness intervention, forgiveness is an ego event. It is not an emotional event. It is a psychological deed conducted with intention. The forgiver *Willfully* insists, "I no longer require you to suffer the way you made me suffer."

5. Following forgiveness, healing is sought. This is because the wound remains. After the person forgives, the therapist must remember to minister to their hurt soul and pray that the anger, shame, rejection, etc. that the person sustained from being trespassed against finds healing through God's grace. This is important.

The Resurrection Effect

Research studies support the notion that forgiveness can contribute powerfully to psychological healing and well-being. Science may well establish that forgiveness consistently produces a healing, restorative effect on a variety of outcome measures. I observe this to be the case clinically. I believe that the restoration of mental health that forgiveness almost inevitably produces is an effect of forgiveness. Because forgiveness so powerfully lifts souls to the experience of new psychological life, I call this effect *The Resurrection Effect.*

An example of *The Resurrection Effect* exists in the experience of Joseph Cardinal Bernardin (1997). Bernardin was falsely accused of sexually abusing a former seminarian. Before the world, he was maligned in the media. Due to the plethora of sexual scandals among clergy, many doubted when the Cardinal denied the charges. Bernardin knew this, and he saw himself being ruined and maligned, all unjustly, by this false accusation. Bernardin experienced a great trespass. But, finally, the man who accused him admitted that he had lied. Cardinal Bernardin met with this young man and forgave him for accusing him falsely. Cardinal Bernardin did not file libel charges against him. Nor did he tongue-lash him. He did not demand anything. He formally substituted a *Will to Forgive* him over the *Will to Punish* him. He forgave him, and then he celebrated Mass for him. He gave him Our Lord. Listen to what the late Cardinal wrote in his autobiography:

Never in my entire priesthood have I witnessed a more powerful reconciliation. The words I am using to tell you this story cannot describe the
power of God's grace at work that afternoon. It was a manifestation of
God's love, forgiveness, and healing that I will never forget .... As [I]
flew back to Chicago that evening, I felt the lightness of spirit that ...
grace brings to one's life (p. 39-40).

This is a wonderful example of the *Resurrection Effect*: a psychological
healing complemented by lightness of spirit. What happened to Bernardin
can happen for all of us.

Social science has just begun to understand that forgiving our trespassers
is imperative to psychological health—an imperative that Jesus of Nazareth
understood two thousand years ago—an imperative that culminates in the
psychological healing and the ebullience characteristic of *The Resurrection
Effect*.

The Imperative to Forgive: What Jesus Taught
There can be no doubt that Jesus taught radical forgiveness. The Gospels
disclose his unambiguous teachings about the matter. Jesus tells Peter to forgive the brother who wrongs him seventy-seven times (Mt. 18:21-22, *"70
times 7 times" in some translations*), essentially commanding forgiveness
for every offense. In the Lord's Prayer, Jesus teaches us to forgive the sins,
while praying to the Father, of "those who are in debt to us" (Mt. 6:12) from
their wrong treatment of us. Also, Jesus tells us to "forgive others their failings" (Mt. 6:14) and to "forgive whatever you have against anybody" (Mk
11:25). His position is unmistakable. Forgive. Forgive. Forgive. Jesus commands us to forgive.

A Psychological Exegesis of Jesus' Command To Forgive:
Suffering Hurt, The Damaged Psyche and
The *Will to Punish* Imprisoning Us in Complexes
Why does Jesus teach us to forgive so unequivocally? What did Jesus of
Nazareth know about mental and spiritual health that makes forgiveness so
imperative? What about his teaching frees us to experience *The Resurrection
Effect*?

The teachings of Jesus of Nazareth inform the psychology of healing
Core Wounds and related problems. In this regard, Our Lord's teachings
from Mt. 5:21-26 are immeasurably helpful.

When someone is sinned against, they sustain a psychic wound. The
wound is a crack in the wholeness and dynamic functioning that is the Divine *Imago* within them. The psychic wound sustained by the trespass ob-
scures the inner harmony that is one's birthright as a child of God, while giving rise to intellectual, emotional, behavioral, somatic, and spiritual dysfunc-

**Jesus teaches that the *Will to Punish* the offender
locks one into one's woundedness. The very desire
to punish the offender, punishes the punisher
by locking the psychic woundedness
into an internal prison. Once in this prison,
the woundedness configured in the *Core Wound*
is unavailable to the healing properties
of either natural or supernatural grace ...
The *Will to Punish* is analogous to a jailhouse wall
that locks in the *Core Wound*
and locks out God's healing**

tion. The pain of having the *Imago* obscured next gives rise to highly charged affects, like anger and resentment. These affects formulate, consciously or unconsciously within the psyche, into a *Will to Punish* which is directed at the offender. Now the trouble begins. Jesus teaches that the *Will to Punish* the offender locks one into one's woundedness. The very desire to punish the offender, punishes the punisher by locking their psychic woundedness into an internal prison. Once in this prison, the woundedness configured in the *Core Wound* is unavailable to the healing properties of either natural or supernatural grace. The *Will to Punish* walls out the mind's native tendency to heal as well as God's healing movement toward the wound. If someone experiences betrayal, for example a child abused and neglected by a parent, and develops a *Will to Punish* the betrayer, the *Core Wound* caused by the betrayal will operate virtually imprisoned within the psyche. The *Will to Punish* is analogous to a jailhouse wall that locks in the *Core Wound* and locks out God's healing.

Jesus explains it this way,

> Anyone who is angry with a brother will answer for it before the court; and anyone who calls a brother "Fool" will answer for it before the Sanhedrin; and anyone who calls him "Traitor" will answer for it in hellfire (Mt. 5:22-23).

In this section of the gospel, Jesus maps out a scenario wherein the plaintiff experiences anger at another for suffering an offense that has distinguished the offender in the mind of the plaintiff as a "Fool" and a "Traitor." When the plaintiff, however, seeks from the court a just punishment for the person who wronged him, the plaintiff himself oddly experiences punishment.

One explanation for the plaintiff/accuser suffering punishment rather than receiving satisfaction by seeing the Fool/Traitor punished is that the plaintiff is unconscious of having criminally sinned against the one he accuses. Unaware that his offense is greater than the Fool/Traitor's offense against him, he remains unconscious of impending court judgment against him. While this interpretation appears valid in and of itself, it does not help us to understand the teaching in light of Jesus' other statements, telling us to forgive over and over, even when as is the case in Peter's question, the question of forgiveness is not qualified by the plaintiff's having participated in wrong doing.

Others make us angry, Jesus teaches, because they treat us in a sinful way. Yet, when we develop a *Will to Punish* our offenders, we imprison ourselves in our unforgiveness. When we want to punish others for the sins they commit against us, it is as though our own *Will to Punish* becomes a prison that locks out God's healing grace from the hurt within our soul, while imprisoning the wound itself in the core of our psyche.

In the case, for example, of a child who suffers the parental treason of neglect or abuse, a *Will to Punish* the offending parent will harm the child's ability to heal from the parent's sin. The *Will to Punish* the offending parent *locks in* the wound of painful lovelessness and the painful anger at the injustice. At the same time, the *Will to Punish* will also *lock out* God's healing grace that would restore love to the child's core and thus heal the wound.

Jesus of Nazareth—an expert in restoring the *Imago* to the human psyche—tells psychological captives how to gain freedom. Jesus knew that the extent to which one maintains the *Will to Punish*, one maintains the woundedness in the *Core Wound* sustained by the wrong suffered. Hence Jesus taught:

> "And when you stand in prayer, forgive whatever you have against anybody, so that your Father in heaven may forgive you your failings too" (Mk. 11:25).

If we think of "failings" as anything outside of the Image of God, like our wounds and complexes sustained from other's sins against us, we see that Jesus offers us a way to heal these "failings." By forgiving others, we abandon the *Will to Punish* which imprisons us in our woundedness. Based on our ego's response to Jesus' teaching, we willingly and willfully assert a *Will to Forgive*. Forgiveness begins as an act of will. It is an intention, a resolution based firmly within the ego's freedom to respond to Jesus' command to forgive enemies. The *Will to Forgive* is an intention based squarely upon the ego's resolve to follow Christ, despite the contrary retributive stance of the wounded psyche. It removes the prison wall. Once accomplished, no barrier exists to impede healing grace. *Core Wounds* can heal, because the *Will to Punish* no longer locks out the God of healing. The *Imago* can be restored.

The Clinical Process: The Road to *The Resurrection Effect*

The road to *The Resurrection Effect* through forgiveness takes place in three clinical stages:

1. problem definition
2. psycho-spiritual education
3. healing prayer.

Stage one involves defining the problem. When in the course of therapy, clients discover that they have been hurt by others, the difficult work begins. In this stage, the therapeutic goal consists in establishing who hurt them (e.g. parent, friend, authority figure), how they were hurt (e.g. neglect, abuse, omission, commission), and how the hurt took up residence in the psyche as dynamics of dysfunction arising from the *Core Wound* (e.g. clinical syndrome, characterological flaws). This stage of treatment establishes that someone sinned against the client, that the sin caused lasting harm, and that the *Will to Punish* the offender exists. Stage one concludes with anger available to the client's ego.

Stage two is terribly important. It pivots the client from a state of unawareness about how to heal from other-inflicted wounds to an awareness of deep psychological healing opportunities inherent in Jesus' teaching about forgiveness. It personalizes *The Resurrection Effect*. During this stage the therapist and the client discuss relevant principles from Matthew chapter 5 and other germane scripture. Further discussed is how the *Will to Punish* imprisons the client's woundedness and the emergent dysfunction within the client's psychic system. A crucial therapeutic task involves validating the reasonableness of the client's *Will to Punish*, establishing that—given the present state of human nature—the *Will to Punish* trespassers intuitively feels like the psyche's most right response. Psychospiritual education establishes that the retributive stance feels most natural but is not in the client's best interests, when considered in the light of the Son of Man's higher understanding of human nature. During this stage, two-fold goals include:

- developing an intellectual understanding of how the retributive stance locks in woundedness and
- that a *Will to Forgive* can replace the *Will to Punish* and remove barriers to natural and supernatural healing grace.

Stage two concludes with the client ready to commit spiritual deeds based on Jesus' teachings: to forgive, and to experience *The Resurrection Effect.*

Stage three involves the actual business of forgiving and healing. At this stage, prayer represents the principal therapeutic intervention. This stage of therapy brings to mind Jesus' words in Matthew 5:23-24,

... if you are bringing your offering to the altar and there remember that

... the client willingly and willfully asserts before God that his or her intentions toward the persecutor have changed. They revise their *Will* and assert that the person in debt to them no longer owes them a debt of equal woundedness.

your brother has something against you, leave your offering there before the altar, go and be reconciled with your brother first, and then come back and present your offering.

Jesus says that prayer will become efficacious to the extent that reconciliation—but for our purposes *forgiveness*, a component of reconciliation—occurs. Forgive the person who hurt you before you pray for the hurt that was caused. Then the prayer for healing will be efficacious. This dynamic guides the healing prayer.

The prayer itself has several components. My client and I picture ourselves going to the client's inner altar to pray for healing of a psychic wound, a *Core Wound*. Then we recall that the prayer for inner healing may not be effective, because forgiveness of the trespasser has not yet occurred. We leave our prayer intention for inner healing at the inner altar and go to the place in the client's psyche where the *Will to Punish* exists. Then, still in prayer, the client willingly and willfully asserts before God that his or her intentions toward the persecutor have changed. They revise their *Will* and assert that the person in debt to them no longer owes them a debt of equal woundedness. When the client asserts the *Will to Forgive* over the *Will to Punish* before God, the barrier of unforgiveness drops away. God's healing grace is no longer locked out, and the woundedness is no longer locked in. This prayer springs the *Core Wound* from its inner prison. Next, the prayer involves the client returning to the inner altar and making an offering of prayer, praying that God's healing grace will act upon the inner wound inflicted by the one now forgiven. This involves inviting the Holy Spirit in Jesus' name to restore the Image dwelling in the Father's divine imagination for the wounded part of the client. This prayer involves acknowledging that God has something special in mind for that portion of psyche which has been sinned against and wounded. This prayer involves inviting the Trinity to operate upon the wounded area so that the image of that area will conform to God's Image of how that psychological place should thrive.

The following prayer may serve as a sample forgiveness prayer:

Father, I pray in Jesus' name and according to his teachings. I have a wound inside my soul. I intend to offer a prayer for healing of that wound. But Jesus tells me to make peace with those who inflicted this wound upon me before I offer this prayer. When I freely offer forgiveness to those who have hurt me, when I replace my *Will to Punish* them with my *Will to Forgive* them, then I free this wound from the prison of unforgiveness. I am confident that I will experience your healing grace, because no barrier will exist within me to lock out your restorative power.

Thus, Father, in Jesus' name, I will ask you to heal the wound that they inflicted upon me. But, first I leave my prayer intention like an offering on your altar. I proceed to the place within my soul where I see those who harmed me through the following act of Treason and/or Foolishness:_____. Even though they wronged me, I follow the teachings of your son, Jesus Christ. Using my free *Will*, I excuse them of any obligation to me. I no longer require they experience a punishment like the one inflicted upon me. I replace my *Will to Punish* them with a *Will to Forgive* them.

Now that I have made peace with those who hurt me, God, I return to my prayer intention—like a person returning to your altar after making peace with his brother. Lord God, I continue to pray in Jesus' name that you will heal the wound inflicted on me by those I just forgave. I have forgiven them their failings.

Please heal me now of the way their failings have injured me. Please take away the absence-of-love, the anger, the anxiety, the shame, the pain, the deep hurt. Please heal painful ways of thinking, feeling, and behaving that spring from this wound. Please heal me in mind, body, and spirit. Please restore the Image of God to that part of my soul. Thank you for sending the Holy Spirit with your healing grace. In Jesus' name. Amen.

Forgiving our trespassers frees us to receive healing of the wounds they inflicted upon us. Forgiveness leads to freedom. Forgiveness leads to *The Resurrection Effect.*

Case Illustrations
So far I have developed a somewhat abstracted version of *Christian Holism* and its Practical Theology of Forgiveness. In this section, I describe some published stories and clinical case experiences that generated my development of this psychology and theology of forgiveness. These illustrations ground the principals of forgiveness in clinical reality, and depict the road to *The Resurrection Effect* in terms of process. Reporting the case examples with permission from my clients, I have changed some information to preserve confidentiality without compromising the relevant clinical events.

A Captive No Longer

The first case is that of Sgt. Jacob deShazer. A U.S. soldier stationed in the Pacific theater during World War II, deShazer was captured by the Japanese and interred in a concentration camp. Because of his soldierly spirit and his captors' brutality, deShazer developed a hatred for his enemies and cultivated fantasies of slaughtering them.

The Japanese forbade the Americans to practice their religion. So, deShazer, who was not religious, delighted when a Bible was smuggled into the camp. This gave him an opportunity to break the rules and defy his captors by reading it. However, when he read the Gospel where the crucified Christ cries, "Father, forgive them, for they know not what they do," deShazer had a change of heart. Jesus of Nazareth's exemplification of forgiveness "transformed deShazer's thinking .... It reorganized his experience of who he was and who he could be" (McCullough, Sandage, & Worthington, 1997, p. 108). Convinced that Christ's forgiving path exceeded his retributive one, deShazer forgave his captors.

Shortly after his conversion experience—and the forgiveness that characterized his conversion—one of the prison guards intentionally slammed an iron door on deShazer's foot. Suffering physical pain from this cruel act, deShazer witnessed his emotional response with shock. He neither hated the guard nor desired revenge. Even though he was still a prisoner of war held by guards and razor wire, deShazer was no longer confined to a psychological and spiritual prison. Through forgiveness, God freed him from psychospiritual captivity.

The "Touch" of Forgiveness

In her memoir, *Tramp for the Lord* (ten Boom & Buckingham, 1974), Corrie ten Boom credited the love of Jesus Christ with helping her survive a Nazi concentration camp during World War II. After the war, Corrie visited churches and talked about her faith. Following one such talk, a man approached her. Immediately she recognized him as one of the former prison guards, known for his cruelty. To her horror, he extended his hand and asked for her forgiveness.

Corrie was stunned. How could she forgive such a loathsome person— one who had worked in service to the Holocaust—one who had participated in the senseless torture and death of so many people? Because she was preaching the Gospel of Christ and the Gospel of forgiveness, ten Boom decided to make the attempt. Following a quick prayer and acting in faith, she took his hand and forgave him. Corrie then felt God's spiritual power ignite in her heart and radiate to the former Nazi. To her surprise, Corrie found that she suddenly loved the man. Implicit in her description of this forgiveness episode is a comprehensive level of healing both for herself and the transgressor.

Zeb

Zeb was a strapping Christian young man of 27. Recently discharged from a responsible position in the Army, he looked forward to finishing his schooling, assuming a well-paying civilian job, and seeking a wife. Several months out of the service, however, things started to go awry. He noticed that without the highly structured life of a military serviceman, he had trouble making decisions. He postponed applying for school, decided to work for a while instead, then thought the better of it after missing the deadline for applications. With more time on his hands, he accomplished less and less. Living off his savings, he spent his days sitting in his apartment, indecisive about his plans, neglecting to make even simple decisions about daily life. He found himself unable to commit to a course in life.

During this time, Zeb noticed that his thoughts became problematic. When socializing with friends, he found that odd thoughts intruded into his consciousness. Often these thoughts involved harming the person to whom he spoke. During conversation, Zeb found that violent images suddenly sprang to his mind. What would begin as an enjoyable conversation would conclude with Zeb trying desperately to suppress images of striking or spitting on his companions. While he hid his upset, these violent thoughts and images stormed though his mind and significantly impaired his ability to relate to others. Since contact with others seemed to trigger these violent thoughts, Zeb tried to defend himself against the aggressive thoughts by isolating himself. To his dismay, however, a new set of disturbing thoughts intruded into his consciousness. A committed Christian, he was disturbed by blasphemous cognitions and sacrilegious images that seemed to take on a life of their own within his psyche. Zeb recognized his obsessions as unreasonable, but he could not stop thinking these intrusive, tormenting thoughts.

By the time we began our therapeutic relationship, he was under psychiatric care for Obsessive-Compulsive Disorder. While his psychiatrist's prescriptions provided relief of some of the intensity of his troubling thoughts, his obsessions continued to intrude into his consciousness and derail his efforts to put his life on track. Working in conjunction with Zeb's psychiatrist, I offered a variety of cognitive-behavioral techniques, including thought stopping, exposure with response prevention, and Rational Emotive Therapy. Similar to his response to medication, Zeb found that these psychotherapeutic techniques enabled him to cope but did not solve his problem. The intrusive thoughts continued to disturb him.

Several months into treatment, Zeb learned that I was a practicing Episcopalian and that I believed in healing prayer. Excitedly, Zeb confided that he, too, was an Episcopalian and would like me to include healing prayer as part of the treatment. I agreed, and we designated the next several sessions for healing prayer. Both of us entertained high hopes for the prayer interventions, but following several sessions of soaking prayer and intercession no real progress occurred. Although neither of us had lost faith in God's power to heal, we realized that we were probably missing some important piece of information. Acting upon a mutually shared intuition, we agreed to explore Zeb's early life to see if the key to his healing might lie there.

At first, Zeb's recollections of growing up were utterly normal. He recollected a happy home life, plenty of love, and feelings of safety. When we dug deeper, however, we discovered painful memories regarding his father. Zeb's earliest recollection went to the age of four. He recalled his father, tired and ill-tempered after work, sitting in a chair and criticizing his little boy for the way he walked across the living room. Apparently, Zeb's father thought that his son walked incorrectly. Zeb next recalled being a little older and seeking his father's approval for a model airplane he had worked hard to complete. Rather than compliment the achievement, his father roundly criticized Zeb for a number of flaws in the model's execution. Zeb was crushed. Another memory involved an early sports experience. Proud of having been chosen to start in his first organized football game, Zeb played an instrumental role in several touchdowns, but after the game his father only spoke to him about the few mistakes he had made. By exploring these memories and others like it, it became clear that his father never recognized Zeb for his talents or achievements. Zeb acknowledged that while his father's abuses lacked an atrocious quality, they nevertheless malignantly impacted his sensitive psyche.

Based on the above, Zeb and I developed the following case conceptualization: Because Zeb's father had never mentored him, Zeb had never learned to be his own man. When he was in the military, daily life was highly structured and nicely compensated for the indecisiveness that results from the absence of a reliable male role model. Upon discharge, however, the externally imposed military structure left, and Zeb's life stalled, because his father never taught him to activate himself to advance his interests. Additionally, we conceptualized that the violent, intrusive thoughts over which he obsessed and experienced so much distress, stemmed from a deep reservoir of anger, originally directed toward his father, but generalized to any person with whom he became close. It was as if a part of his psyche, despite Zeb's conscious desires, sought to protect him from impending humiliations and rejections he had come to expect through the formative relationship with his father. We further conceptualized that the blasphemous cognitions and sacrilegious images that tormented Zeb, were a transference of the anger Zeb felt toward his humiliating, rejecting earthly father to his heavenly Father. The sacrilegious thoughts that invaded Zeb's mind birthed from the part of Zeb's psyche that believed that God the Father should suffer equal and opposite humiliation that Zeb experienced from his father on earth.

Arriving at these insights inaugurated a heady time in therapy. Zeb and I had worked hard to uncover the secret source of his stalled life and violent, intrusive thoughts. We were certain that when we prayed again for inner healing, we would pray rightly, and therefore effectively. We decided to pray for healing of the humiliation and under-mentoring that represented the *Core Wound* (A *Core Wound* can be thought of as a wound that is central to our very being and manifests as an empty, shattered place in the soul.) of the Father Complex/Schema. Our rationale was that, if the humiliation from his father's constant criticism and rejection healed, then the anger and the reflexively defensive role of the aggressive thoughts and images would have no psychic purpose, causing the *Core Wound* to collapse on itself. Then we would pray for a reconfiguration of the former core of the Father Complex, that God would change the image of the rejected, humiliated son into an image consistent with the Image of God—an image of a beloved son.

After agreeing on issues that our healing prayer needed to address, we spent part of the next therapy session in prayerful intercession. We expected a lot. But nothing happened. Our headiness turned to deflation and discouragement. Zeb struggled with the idea that perhaps God the Father really was as rejecting as his earthly father, and I began to question whether I had made a technical error by incorporating Christian faith into psychotherapy.

During this time of clinical discouragement, I reread The Gospel According to Saint Matthew. After reading the fifth chapter, a cascade of ideas developed that resulted in the rudiments of the theory enumerated above. Applying the theory to Zeb, I began to wonder if our prayer for his inner healing failed because we had not applied Jesus' teachings on forgiveness to the clinical situation. Certainly something blocked the operation of natural and supernatural grace on Zeb's Father Complex and the Obsessive-Compulsive syndrome that arose from it. Some barrier existed that kept God's healing power from the core of Zeb's wounded area. I shared with Zeb my hunch that his Father Complex and his Obsessive-Compulsive syndrome were imprisoned within the *Will to Punish*. In our earlier attempt at healing prayer we had gone to the altar to pray for healing, but we had neglected to leave our healing prayer request at the altar while first making peace with Zeb's father. Making peace with Zeb's father would have meant asserting the *Will to Forgive* over the *Will to Punish*, essentially forgiving just as Jesus commands throughout the gospels. By following Jesus teaching, by forgiving, we would remove the barrier of unforgivenss that kept the wound within Zeb alienated from God's healing grace, and imprisoned the *Core Wound* within him.

Intrigued by the above interpretation, Zeb agreed to formally forgive his father before again praying for inner healing. We used Mt. 5:23-24 as our prayer template. In the clinical setting, we began to pray together. Using the imagery of scripture, we imagined Zeb going to the altar to ask God to heal the rejection and humiliation that was the core of his Father Complex. But, remembering that Zeb held something against his father, we left this prayer intention at the altar and went to the place in Zeb's psyche where he held his father image. There, verbally, out loud, in the presence of God, Zeb acknowledged that, because his father had sinned against him, he had suffered a deep inner wound of humiliation and under-mentoring that gave rise to the symptoms described. Zeb acknowledged that what his father had done was wrong, and it was precisely because it was wrong that Zeb needed to forgive him. In prayer, following the commandments of Christ, Zeb renounced his right and his willingness to have his father suffer in a way equivalent to the suffering he inflicted upon Zeb. In prayer with Zeb, I affirmed that Zeb had just executed Jesus' teaching to forgive. Then, still following the template of Mt. 5:23-24, we returned to the altar to pray for Zeb's inner healing. Taking turns, Zeb and I prayed in Jesus' name to God the Father that God would send the Holy Spirit to heal the different aspects of Zeb's Father Complex, especially the rejection, humiliation and the violent intrusive thoughts that defensively arouse from it, as well as the violent, blasphemous thoughts which represented a defensive position toward the wounding father. We acknowledged in prayer before God that it was Zeb's willing intention that Zeb would forgive his father his failings, just as we hoped that God would forgive Zeb his failings and restore him to the original design inherent in the Image of God. Following this eventful therapy session, we were both somewhat drained. We postponed further processing until the following week.

When Zeb and I next met, he looked like himself, only better. He looked relaxed, happy, and healthy. To an extent, he even glowed. Responding to my question as to what accounted for his looking so well, he unhesitatingly responded, "It's the Holy Spirit. I haven't had a violent or intrusive thought all week. I am in a state of grace. The forgiveness prayer worked." Zeb experienced *The Resurrection Effect*.

We worked together for another three months. During that time, Zeb resumed executing the plans for his life that he had put on hold after he got out of the service. He got a job and resumed a normal social life. Things went well and he experienced a total remission of violent intrusive thoughts for a year. Following a period of stress, he returned to therapy due to a flare-up of intrusive thoughts. In two sessions, these were easily resolved using simple behavioral techniques. Periodically, I hear from him. He continues to live a normal life, to work, to socialize, and to seek love, without the symptoms that brought him into therapy. He believes that forgiving his father in accordance with the teachings of Jesus of Nazareth changed his life and helped him to reclaim his portion of the Image of God within his psyche. He is thankful for *The Resurrection Effect*.

The Forgiveness "Fish"

Another example of the healing power of forgiveness comes from the following case. Importantly, this case involves a brief therapeutic encounter consisting of a one hour contact, followed up by a phone consultation one week later. The fact that the client experienced benefit after brief therapeutic contact suggests that forgiveness may be a treatment of unusual efficacy.

A 35-year-old man sought consultation with me. At the outset of contact, it was clear that he was a high functioning, effective individual. The head of an important non-profit organization, he contributed much to his community and excelled at his philanthropic work. He enjoyed an unusually happy marriage to a pretty, talented wife. Together with her, he was raising two boys, ages 7 and 4. For the weeks prior to consultation, he found himself growing increasingly uneasy. Usually patient with his children, he observed that he responded to their needs and naive mistakes with irritability, down-putting overreaction, and an inappropriate drive to control them. He knew neither the source of this behavior toward his children, nor how to stop acting it out towards them. These episodes culminated in a dream which so disquieted him that the next day he sought my services via phone.

The dream he disclosed to me is as follows: he found himself in the house in which he grew up. The house had fallen into a dilapidated state. He felt that he should abandon it for a newer, more comfortable dwelling. For some reason, however, he was indentured to the house and to his father who strode about the halls of the run-down dwelling. His father ordered him about and demanded that he commence with unreasonably ambitious construction projects. He protested to his father that the shabby dwelling did not warrant such effort, but the father insisted that the son "owed" him the work. His father insisted that the son had an almost legal obligation to pursue the ill-conceived building projects at the father's bidding. When his father ordered him to install expensive fish tanks in the walls of the house, the son went to work, executing the odd request with the hope that this final task would discharge further obligation to his tyrannical dad. Completing this unrewarding task, he approached his father to say his farewell and strike out on his own. To his dismay, however, his father sternly informed him that he would not let him leave until he fulfilled a last duty. The father pointed to the largest fish tank and told his son that he could only be acquitted of his indentured status if he sailed to sea and caught a rare fish and deposited it in the father's tank. Only this would conclude their business and allow the son the to leave his tyrannical father and his dilapidated house. Upon hearing this, the son had a violent physical reaction. His left shoulder hurt, and he found a circular bruise around a red open wound. The pain was excruciating. At the same time he experienced a wave of physical nausea as he anticipated going out to sea in search of the fish and suffering debilitating sea-sickness. The idea of securing the fish for his father was wildly distasteful.

We dove into dream interpretation. During his youth, just as in the dream, this man had experienced his father as denigrating and tyrannical. His dad had wounded his soul. The dream revealed this wound as the unhealed area

The fact that the client experienced benefit after brief therapeutic contact suggests that forgiveness may be a treatment of unusual efficacy.

of his left shoulder. The dilapidated dream house represented the *Core Wound*—the subjective space within which the hurtful experiences with his dad continued to operate and determine his thinking, emotion, and behavior. In his recent adult life, this psychological wound operated in the projection of his hurt childhood self onto his children, with the man acting out the role of his mean dad. In other words, the wounding father/son dynamic operated both within the subjective space of his dream house and within the objective space of his real house. He lamented that he had begun to repeat the painful dynamics of his childhood. He wanted to save his sons from the tyranny he himself had so painfully experienced. His verbalized sentiment that this father/son dynamic was "getting old" consciously expressed the symbolism of the dilapidated house in the dream. The house was old, no longer useful, and not worth even fixing up. He desired to leave his old frame of reference for father/son relationships. The dream, however, showed that something kept pulling him back into the relational dynamics depicted by the dream dad's insistence that the son remained obligated to him. The dream father would not let his son leave the dysfunctional subjective frame of reference, the frame of reference that dictated the man's own troubling responses to his little sons.

At this point, we committed ourselves to exploring if the dream offered a way to freedom. We explored the symbols of his dream in earnest. What kept him in the house with his dad? What would free him? The following insights rewarded our efforts: symbolically, the dream did point the way to a new frame of reference, of getting free from the dilapidated father/son dynamic. Freedom appeared in the form of a fish, given to the dream father. For Christians, dream fish are often emblems of Christ (Lewis, 1995). I believe that the Holy Spirit brought Jesus' teaching in the form of the dream fish to show this man the way to healing and freedom. Jesus taught that the way to spring free from our prisons, to get free from the obligation that imprisons us, is to pay something. "In truth I tell you, you will not get out until you have paid the last penny" (Mt. 5:26). The fish represented a shocking means of healing and freedom to this man that was utterly consistent with his Christianity. To heal, he had to let his father "off the hook." He had to surrender his *Will to Punish* his father. He had to forgive his dad for inflicting the psychological wound symbolized in the festering shoulder. The man's desire to take from his father in punishment for what the father had taken from him via a tyrannical upbringing had to be surrendered back to the offensive father. By forgiving his father's debt to him, he pays out to his father the punishment that his father owes him. In short, the fish represents the forgiveness that Jesus of Nazareth taught us to give to those who trespass against us. Carrying out Christ's teaching, however, is hard to the point of being sickening. The *Will to Punish* is intuitive and native to human psychological impulses, while the *Will to Forgive* is not. Note that when the dream father asserted that he would discharge his son from him and the subjective space associated with him, if the son would give back what he intended to take from the dream father, the son became nauseous. The man saw that the prospect of fishing the *Will to Forgive* out of his soul sickened him.

At this point in the consultation, he became agitated and complained that his muscles had tensed to a painful level of constriction. The idea of replacing the *Will to Punish* with the *Will to Forgive* was obviously painful. But, being a man of faith and courage, he resolved to pray a prayer of forgiveness for his father and let him off the hook. Then, our consultation period concluded, and we set up a phone meeting for the following week.

During the interim, I reflected that our brief consult had fruitfully passed through the first two stages of the forgiveness model. One, this man's intelligence and sensitivity to his psychological life, aided by an innate gift for understanding his dreams, led to a level of problem definition and psychological understanding that was unusually thorough, despite the complexity of the psychodynamics and the brevity of our consultation. Second, he quickly grasped the importance of forgiveness as the key to freeing him from the unfortunate relations he had with his sons, and he concluded the session resolving to follow Jesus' teaching in the matter, rather than to allow his natural revulsion to forgiveness compromise his hope for freedom in father/son relations. He resolved to forgive his father, not only to heal himself, but to save his little sons from a similar fate.

When he contacted me a week later, he informed that he had prayed according to the Matthew prayer protocol and that his revulsion about forgiving his father rapidly receded into a sense of relief. Further, he noticed that interacting with his own sons had become far less problematic than before he forgave his father. Now, he informed me, he found that he could easily stop denigrating or tyrannical behavior toward his sons. Had this man been available for more treatment, we would have devoted more therapy and prayer to aggressively reversing the damage of his childhood. But his renewed emotional equilibrium, behavioral control, and intellectual awareness demonstrate that this man enjoyed some of beneficial outcomes often associated with *The Resurrection Effect*. Had he had time for more forgiveness work, I believe that he would have healed even more.

Sylvia

This next case is of interest to anyone interested to learn how forgiveness work can effectively treat clinical syndromes and the deep psychological

This ... case is of interest to anyone interested to learn how forgiveness work can effectively treat clinical syndromes and the deep psychological wounds that underlie them.

wounds that underlie them.

A 33-year-old physician, Sylvia, sought consultation, concerned that she had "not been herself" for a year. A year previously, she had diagnosed a 14 year old girl with a serious illness. While treating her young patient, she had become restless, keyed up, physically tense, and unable to sleep well. Try as Sylvia might, she could not calm herself and regain her former happiness. Due to her medical training, she was savvy regarding psychiatric matters. She diagnosed herself with Generalized Anxiety Disorder and, deciding against pharmaceutical intervention, sought psychotherapy.

After speedily building rapport, we began an aggressive regimen of cognitive and behavioral interventions. Cognitively, we pursued the notion that Generalized Anxiety stems from the tendency to over-interpret life's events in terms of a personal threat. We worked at disputing irrational, anxiety provoking thoughts as they automatically popped into Sylvia's mind and replaced these with reality-based, safety-oriented thoughts. Behaviorally, we pursued stress reduction techniques geared to short-circuit the fight/flight response with the relaxation response. While Sylvia performed these exercises and was formally good at them, she gained little real relief.

Experiencing frustration, we decided to look into her early life to see if we could find the historical root of her anxiety. As Sylvia told her story, my heart went out to her. She was the younger of two sisters. Shortly after Sylvia's birth, her father died, leaving Sylvia's grief-stricken mother to succumb to alcoholism before Sylvia had reached the age of 5. Early on, Sylvia demonstrated exceptional intelligence, and it fell to her to meet her sister's psychological and maternal needs, and it also fell to her to clean up after her mother's drinking.

When Sylvia reached the age of 10, a local minister helped her mother find sobriety. No longer drinking, Sylvia's mother threw herself into nurturing her daughters. For a time, Sylvia thrived on her mother's attention. The unhappy years of her stolen childhood, she hoped, would be restored in a puberty and adolescence complete with her mom's loving nurturing. Such relief. Such happiness. But the relief and happiness were short lived.

One day after school, scampering home to bake cookies with her mom, Sylvia found her mother crying at the kitchen table. The family doctor, Sylvia's mother wept, had just diagnosed Sylvia's sister with a serious disease. But Sylvia's mom was determined to keep her eldest daughter alive. When Sylvia saw her mother devote herself to her ill sister's complicated care, she feared that her mother might resume drinking. She did not. Rather, she cared for Sylvia's sister admirably. In fact, to Sylvia's horror, her mother devoted so much energy to Sylvia's sick sister, that she had nothing left for Sylvia. The poor girl was bitterly hurt. To her, the situation was crazily unjust. Not only had Sylvia surrendered her childhood to her mother's alcoholism, but now, just when she had begun to recover her longed-for mother's love, her sister robbed it from Sylvia, monopolizing her mother's love by illness. At the core, Sylvia was stunned with hurt. Her mother hurt her by abandoning her a second time. Her sister hurt her by stealing the love she so badly needed to flourish. Anger and resentment built up around her hurt core.

On some level, she wished her mother to hurt as she hurt. On another level she wished that her sister would die, both to punish her for robbing away mother's love, and as a wish-fulfillment-means of removing her sister as an obstruction to her mother's attention. Because Sylvia was "supposed" to be the helpful kid without needs, no one ever processed Sylvia's hurt or anger with her at the early age. Sylvia herself, did not feel entitled to her hurt or anger, so her pain and her *Will to Punish* went underground. She threw herself into her role as the helpful one, a role that dominated her life and culminated in becoming a physician. But in the previous year, when she diagnosed and began treatment of the sick 14 year old girl, the events were too similar to the trauma of her sister's illness. Her *Core Wound* activated. She felt chronic global anxiety, because the destructive emotions connected to her *Will to Punish* dangerously threatened her entrenched self-image of helper and healer.

A Christian, Sylvia was intrigued by the model of forgiveness that I presented. Before immediately praying the forgiveness prayer, however, we spent several sessions gathering Sylvia's anger at her mother and sister. Neither of us were interested in compromising the therapy by praying a prayer of forgiveness before Sylvia's anger was fully available to her ego. In itself, this part of the therapy contributed to causing her anxiety to collapse, because making her anger conscious negated the need to defend against its emergence with physiological arousal and emotional dread. With the *Will to Punish* out of the unconscious, her forgiveness of her mother and sister would be meaningful and real. Most importantly, forgiveness would clear away the psychological barriers to the Holy Spirit's desire to heal the deep wound of early neglect.

Finally, we prayed in the usual way. We prayed to God in the name of Jesus Christ that our intention was to have the deep hurt caused by her mother and sister healed, but we left this prayer request at the altar of Sylvia's healing intention, and went to that place in her psyche where she maintained the *Will to Punish* her mother and sister. During this part of the prayer, she formally renounced the *Will to Punish* them and asserted the *Will to Forgive* them. As soon as Sylvia prayed this part of the prayer, an intense feeling of being in the presence of an incredibly powerful Spirit of Love came over us both. It seemed to fill my entire office. Both of us were over-whelmed in the presence of the Holy Spirit. We had difficulty speaking, be-cause the Holy Spirit's love and beauty moved us to tears. We struggled to finish the prayer by simply reiterating our original prayer intention, that the painful absence of love at her core would be replaced by God's restorative, healing love. Done praying, we sat in the midst of the awesome presence. It was so beautiful and powerful and loving, I had the impression that the walls of my office would strain by the force of God's passionate love and explode.

For Sylvia, the outcome was excellent. For two weeks, she had wonderful dreams and a feeling of deep goodness and energy at her core. When she came down from her "high", she experienced full remission of the anxiety that brought her to treatment. Even more wonderfully, she reported that the hurt connected with her *Core Wound* had simply been healed by the love of God. Her experience is consistent with *The Resurrection Effect.*

Bereavement and Constipation

A client came to me who initially asked for psychotherapy for what ap-peared to be complicated bereavement. She simply could not get over the death of her husband. In life, her husband had been in the 1st Gulf War and, as the result of his combat experience, had tremendous Post Traumatic Stress Disorder (PTSD). To medicate this, he used drugs and alcohol for years. Fi-nally, he got treatment, received healing and became a counselor himself, in fact, a very good one. He met this much younger woman at an Episcopal church and they married. She was very happy in the marriage. When he died, she was devastated. In therapy, we kept praying that this complicated be-reavement would heal, but it just did not happen. No matter what interven-tion we tried—spiritual or psychological—nothing seemed to help.

Eventually, it became clear that she was angry at him for taking such poor care of his body after the war. She was thinking: "How dare you send your-self to an early grave and leave me here. You ruined yourself on drugs. I was happy with you. Your post-war drug use led to your death." Even though she loved him, she was furious at him and had an unconscious *Will to Punish* him. Then we prayed that she would forgive him for taking such poor care of himself, and she asserted the *Will to Forgive*, saying "I will no longer ask you to suffer the way you made me suffer. I forgive you for the drug abuse and for dying because of it." We then went back and prayed to God to heal from her complicated bereavement, and God healed it.

After that healing took place, a whole new level of woundedness came forward. She had a father wound. When she was a child, her father—a high level business man who worked his way up from poverty—did many cruel things to her. In fact, whenever she was around her father, even as an adult, she felt physically small and afraid of him. She was always trying to get him to bless her so that there would be some love placed in her rejected heart, but her father would not love her in the way she needed. It did not surprise me, because, as she grew up, this tremendously selfish father would do outrageous things that would psychologically injure his children. For example, he complained that when his daughter would use the toilet, her flushing made too much noise, was hard on the plumbing and would disturb his rest. Eventually, it got so bad that this poor young girl started going to the bathroom on newspaper like the family dog.

We worked on forgiveness again. As we did, the anger at her Dad for being so tremendously selfish and rejecting became available to her ego. We decided to pray for healing of her wounds in this situation. First, however, during prayer, she forgave her dad for the litany of trespasses he committed against her. Then she prayed for healing of the wounds he inflicted by those trespasses.

Several things happened as a result of this prayer. The most striking result was that the next time she visited her father, even though he berated her as usual, she felt like an adult, and she looked at him and saw a little child—a mean little child. She even found her dad to be sort of comical. The abandonment depression was healed, and she was better able to relate to men.

However, to me the most interesting aspect of this case was psychosomatic. Recall her childhood bathroom trauma. A week after the forgiveness intervention, she came dancing into my office, and the first thing she said to me was: "Dr. Zeiders, I can go to the bathroom!" She had been chronically constipated throughout her adult life and that was now healed.

Loretta

We (my wonderful colleague Julie Wegryn and I) began co-therapy with Loretta. We met one time per week for six months. Some cognitive-behavioral interventions were offered, but we also engaged in psycho-dynamic-style uncovering. Once her story was told, we brainstormed as to how the forgiveness prayer might help her. Eventually, treatment culminated in the forgiveness prayer. We offered prayers throughout therapy and conducted all interventions in the name of Jesus Christ. (Because Loretta's case is so illustrative, I have decided to treat it with special attention.)

1. Client History: Familial and Psychological Dynamics

Family-of-origin issues formed the *Core Wound* that set forth so much unhappiness in her life. Her father was a highly placed official in a religious denomination. In early memories, Loretta recollects him admonishing that God's will for her life was to serve the nuclear family. God expected her, he told her, to put herself last and to take care of her mother and her two younger brothers. Fearing her father's and God's punishment if she disobeyed, she became *good* as good had been inflicted upon her. Instead of loving her in a way that would invigorate the core of her psyche with energy, her father abandoned that part of her to emptiness and indoctrinated her to a life of slavish service to her family.

Her mother played a similar role. Physically frail, lazy, and hypochondriacal, Loretta's mother never expended herself to praise Loretta. Rather, she sought to draw love, nurturing, and reassurance from Loretta, using her alleged sicknesses as the excuse for demanding that Loretta *mother* her. At one point, she told Loretta that unless Loretta fully obeyed, her mother might become so upset that she would die. Hence, Loretta associated any demands she might make on her mother—whether through disobedience or asking for nurturing—as threats to her mother's life.

Both parents insisted that Loretta take parental-like responsibility for her younger brothers. This role as pseudo-parent set forth an ongoing childhood nightmare for Loretta. The younger brothers intuitively understood that although Loretta had responsibility for them, she had no authority over them. Their sadism caused them to delight in setting her up to fail.

On Sundays, Loretta had to prepare her little brothers for church. Her father made it clear that this chore was one of her Christian duties. Not to fulfill it would let God down and open her to verbal abuse and *guilt-tripping* by her religious father. Her mother made it clear that she herself was too frail to dress the boys. Loretta had to dress them to prevent her mother from exhaustion. Under such pressure, Loretta would try to dress her little brothers. She would lay out their clothes and ask them to get dressed for church. Invariably, they would refuse to dress, throwing their clothes out windows and screaming when Loretta tried to correct them. They would run to the parents and accuse Loretta of wild injustice toward them. Loretta's father would blame and shame her for her failure to carry out God's work with her little brothers. Her mother would swoon, look troubled and frail, declaring that Loretta would be the death of her.

This family dynamic repeated itself throughout Loretta's childhood, adolescence, and adulthood. She recalled times that her brothers made poor investments. It then fell to her to give them money. They asked for loans as though they were entitled to them, but never repaid Loretta. At other times, when they asked for and acted on her advice, they never thanked her for good outcomes. When they thought that her advice was poor they denigrated her relentlessly.

When Loretta was a young mother involved in caring for her little children, she received a call from her youngest brother. He demanded that Loretta drop everything and immediately fly to the city where his wife was giving birth to their first child. Loretta was the only one, he exclaimed, who knew how to take care of children. At great personal sacrifice, Loretta honored her brother's request. She bundled up her infant children. She bought plane tickets. And, because her husband had to work, she flew alone to her brother and sister-in-law's to help them with their new infant. When she arrived, she found them extremely stressed from the new responsibility of parenthood. Despite her kindness, they scapegoated her for not arriving even sooner to help them. They also established humiliating house rules to which they told Loretta she would have to abide. Even in the face of their meanness, Loretta helped her nervous brother and sister-in-law. She helped them tremendously and selflessly, but they never thanked her. Even after their children were grown, they would allude to Loretta's visit as though she had done something slightly wrong to them.

Fortunately, Loretta married a kind, supportive man. He sought the best for his wife. He encouraged her to make friends outside of her family. He hoped that the establishment of a positive peer group would help Loretta find happier relationships. Unfortunately, this was not the case. Loretta found herself in relational dynamics very similar to the dynamics she experienced in her family-of-origin. For example, she reached out to a group of ladies in her church. At first, she got along well with them. So well, in fact, that they elected her to become the head of the growth committee. Then similar dynamics unfolded that reiterated the dynamics of her excruciating childhood Sunday mornings trying to dress her brothers. The church growth committee loaded Loretta with great responsibility but they provided her with little authority. When Loretta tried to make necessary changes, her *friends* on the committee rebelled and went to the pastor, complaining that Loretta was unreasonable. In turn, the pastor *guilt-tripped* Loretta and told her that she would be the death of the church. The dysfunctional dynamics of childhood haunted her adult relatinships.

Listening to Loretta tell the story of these experiences, we learned of the emotional toll that was taken on her. For long periods throughout her life, she experienced a depressive emptiness at the core of her being. Also, much of the time she felt shame, as though there was something intrinsically wrong with her. She also had a vague awareness that her relations with her brothers were not right, but she could not help herself from getting into the same humiliating relations with them over and over. Lastly, despite her good marriage, she felt very lonely for a friend. All this emotional and relational pain was exacerbated by progressively debilitating leg pain that doctors attributed to arthritis.

Loretta told these things to us in treatment and our hearts went out to her. We conducted treatment and prayed. We developed a passion to understand the deep structure of her woundedness and to look to God for help in healing Loretta.

As Loretta's story unfolded, we found the following structure within her woundedness: From the beginning her parents rejected her. Obsessed with making Loretta do the *right* and *Christian* thing, Loretta's father had neglected to love his daughter. Similarly, Loretta's mother, neurotically striving to avoid her maternal responsibilities, used her hypochondriacal defenses to shirk her role as a nurturer. She forced Loretta to raise herself and her little brothers. She forced Loretta's compliance by telling Loretta that non-compliance with the situation would kill her. Instead of loving Loretta, both parents abandoned her. When children are abandoned, they often grow into adults who experience emptiness at the core. This was Loretta's case. She also felt anger for being trespassed against by her parents, but she had to bring the anger back upon herself, because she had been indoctrinated that anger at her parents—and the *Will to Punish* that naturally arises from it—made her *bad* to her father and *murderous* to her mother. By turning such vitality—the vitality of anger—back upon herself she developed depression within her emptiness.

Next, the relationship her parents forced her to have with her brothers was especially damaging. Loretta was told that she had to meet the needs of her unappreciative brothers. In this way, she could be good in her father's eyes and keep her mother alive. Because her father's approval and her mother's life were contingent upon Loretta serving her sadistic, immature brothers, this relationship style became the only way that Loretta learned to relate to others. It followed her throughout her life. Each time Loretta repeated this relational dynamic, she experienced another wound that exacerbated the pain in her core. This repetition compulsion determined her relationship with the church growth committee and her pastor. She was compelled to repeat the relational dynamics of her childhood. In all these experiences, the loveless-ness of the relational dynamics kept her core empty, and the anger she turned back upon herself kept her in a state of depression. (Loretta agreed with these interpretations. They modeled reality as she understood it. All of us agreed, however, that only God sees the entire picture, and that none of us really understood the moral or spiritual nature of those who had hurt Loretta in an ultimate sense. God, not ourselves, is the final authority.)

2. Specific Healing Interventions

Loretta wanted to be free from wounded, painful relationships. To meet her need, we discussed Jesus' teaching regarding how unforgiveness locks in our woundedness and how forgiveness frees us for healing. We further proposed that we had gathered enough information about Loretta's past to move to the next decisive stage of healing: the forgiveness prayer. Anxious to heal, Loretta readily agreed.

We opened the prayer in Jesus' name. Then we approached God with the prayer intention that God would heal Loretta from the emptiness and depression she felt and that he would free her from the abusive relational dynamics that plagued her. Recalling, however, that Loretta had outstanding business with those who had trespassed against her, we left these prayer intentions for healing and went to the place within her where she maintained the *Will to*

Punish her father. She replaced her *Will to Punish* him for indoctrinating her to be the family slave with the *Will to Forgive* him for this sin against her. She did the same thing with her mother for not nurturing her and for forcing her to take over the role of mother to her brothers. She then forgave her brothers for the way they wounded her by abusing her nurturing and for their sadism and lack of appreciation. She then began to replace the *Will to Punish* with the *Will to Forgive* regarding other people in her life with whom she had experienced similar hurtful dynamics—including the ladies from the church growth committee and her pastor. Still in prayer, we returned to the original prayer intention. Having forgiven those who trespassed against her, Loretta had, by using her *Will to Forgive*, freed herself from the unforgiveness that blocked out the healing power of the Holy Spirit from the wounds that others had inflicted upon her. We acknowledged that Loretta had forgiven others their failings, just as Jesus had taught. We asked God to now heal Loretta of the way those failings had harmed her soul.

When we concluded this prayer, it was obvious that the clinical situation had entered into a state of unusual grace. The feeling of joy and energy that accompanies the special presence of the Holy Spirit permeated our office. Loretta left feeling encouraged. And she continued the forgiveness prayer. On her drive home, she reported, she had the impression that the Holy Spirit was bringing different people to mind who had injured her psyche. In prayer, she replaced her *Will to Punish* these people with the *Will to Forgive* them. Then she asked the Father in Jesus' name to send the Holy Spirit to heal the part of her soul that had sustained damage from those who had sinned against her.

3. Therapeutic Process

By this time, Loretta had been in therapy for six months. Within four months, she had finished the bulk of stage one, the stage of problem definition. In less than a month, she finished stage two, the stage of developing an intellectual understanding of how forgiving her trespassers could lead to healing. The rest of her sessions were spent praying the forgiveness prayer and discussing outcomes. The outcomes themselves were staggering. Within a very short period of time, Loretta experienced a radical decrease in her experience of inner emptiness and depression. Within five weeks of practicing the forgiveness prayer, Loretta noticed that she had not experienced her repetition compulsion. She found that in none of her relationships had she fallen into the care-take-until-abuse dynamic that plagued and hurt her throughout her life. Following her forgiveness work, she developed a spontaneous ability to avoid the old dynamic and to draw boundaries. She delighted in suddenly finding herself appropriately assertive. Further, just following her forgiveness work, she began a friendship with a woman in her church. Loretta found the experience of friendship delightful. Rather than giving to another while waiting to be abused, Loretta had the first intimate relationship with another person (outside her marriage) that was character- ized by respect and reciprocity. Finally, the pain Loretta had in her leg— originally attributed to arthritis—diminished by 85%, according to Loretta's self-report. All these breakthroughs occurred following the initial forgive- ness prayer and Loretta's ongoing discipline of practicing it.

Because Loretta experienced such profound relief and experienced a wel- come elevation to an energized sense of well being, she was a beneficiary of the *Resurrection Effect*.

Conclusion

Jesus Christ teaches us to forgive. Contained within his teaching is a depth psychology that organizes spiritual and psychological dynamics in such a way that God's grace heals our deepest wounds. By replacing the *Will to Punish* with the *Will to Forgive*, we use our free will to destroy the psy- chological barriers that prevent God's healing grace from healing our *Core Wounds*. When we forgive those who hurt us, we then can pray effectively for the wounds that have been inflicted upon us. God heals us. He enters the wound and restores to it the Image of God. I call this is *The Resurrection Effect.*

Reference Note

1. Dr. Enright, an important forgiveness researcher, has an interesting personal story. He began researching forgiveness as an agnostic, looking for a way to gain grant money and pursue interesting science. He was not particularly reli- gious or spiritual. However, once he began doing this research, he had a conver- sion experience. He is now a practicing Christian, attends church weekly and is fully ensconced in the Christian faith. He is also an amazingly generous, engag- ing man. By scientifically studying the teachings of Jesus of Nazareth, he en- tered Christendom! What a wonderful way to embrace Christianity! We do not have to be scared of the scientific method. It can lead us to the Beautiful Mys- tery.

References

Al-Mabuk, R.H., Enright, R.D., and Cardis, P.A. (1995). Forgiveness education with parentally love-deprived late adolescents. *Journal of Moral Education, 24,* 427- 444. (From McCullough, M., Exline, J., and Baumeister, R. (1998). An annotated bibliography of research on forgiveness and related topics. In E. Worthington (Ed.), *Dimensions of forgiveness: Psychological research and theological perspectives.* Philadelphia, PA: Templeton Foundation Press; subsequently this text will be re- ferred to as McCullough, Exline, et. al.)

Aponte, H. (1998). Love, the spiritual wellspring of forgiveness: an example of spirituality in therapy. *Journal of Family Therapy, 20, (1)*, 37-58.

Bernardin, J. (1997). *The gift of peace*. New York: Image Books.

Caine, W., & Kaufman, B. (1999). *Prayer, faith, and healing.* Emmaus, PA: Rodale Press.

Coyle, C.T., & Enright, R.D. (1997). Forgiveness interventions with post-abortion men. *Journal of Consulting and Clinical Psychology, 65,* 1042-1045. (From McCullough, Exline, et. al.)

Freedman, S.R., and Enright, R.D. (1996). Forgiveness as an intervention goal with incest survivors. *Journal of Consulting and Clinical Psychology, 64,* 983-992.

Hebl, J.H., & Enright, R.D. (1993). Forgiveness as a psychotherapeutic tool with elderly females. *Psychotherapy, 30,* 658-667. (From McCullough, Exline, et. al.)

Lewis, J.R. (1995). *The dream encyclopedia.* Washington, D.C.: Visible Ink.

McCullough, M., Exline, J., and Baumeister, R. (1998). An annotated bibliography of research on forgiveness and related topics. In E. Worthington (Ed.), *Dimensions of forgiveness: Psychological research and theological perspectives.* Philadelphia, PA: Templeton Foundation Press; subsequently this text will be referred to as McCullough, Exline, et. al.

McCullough, M., Sandage, S., & Worthington, E. (1997). *To forgive is human: How to put your past in the past.* Downers Grove, IL: InterVarsity Press.

Poloma, M.M., & Gallup, G.H. (1991). Unless you forgive others. *Varieties of prayer.* Philadelphia, PA: Trinity Press. (From McCullough, Exline, et. al.)

Subkoviak, M.J., Enright, R.D., Woo, C., Gassin, E.A., Freedman, S., Orson, L. M. and Sarinopoulos, I. (1995). Measuring interpersonal forgiveness in late adolescence and middle adulthood. *Journal of Adolescence, 18,* 641-655. (From McCullough, Exline, et. al.)

ten Boom, C. &Buckingham (1974). *Tramp for the Lord.* New York: Jove.

vanOyen Witvliet, C., Ludwig, T., & Vander Laan, K. (2001). Granting forgiveness or harboring grudges: Implications for emotions, physiology, and health." *Psychological Science, Mar; 12(2)*: 117-23.

Wansbrough, H. (Ed.). (1985). *The new Jerusalem bible.* New York: Doubleday.

Worthington, E., Kurusu, T., McCullough, M., & Sandage, S. (1996). Empirical research on religion and psychotherapeutic processes and outcomes: A 10-year review and research prospectus. *Psychological Bulletin, 119,* 448-487.

Zeiders, C., and Schaller, J. (1998). The argument for the inclusion of spirituality. *The Journal of Christian Healing, 20, (1),* 33-45.

Offertory Prayer

We offer to you the persons who have done things to us that have hurt us.

We offer to you those who have oppressed us, slandered us, rejected us, ignored us, misunderstood us, harmed us, attacked us, and done things which we cannot say.

By their real or imagined offenses, we have become wounded. Our thinking has become disordered, our feelings painful, our bodies sick, our experience of life a disappointment.

Father, in the hate and rage we feel toward these people, we avail ourselves of the great dignity we possess as creatures made in the Image of God.

Despite our hurt feelings, thoughts, and bodies, despite the cruel results in us of others' unkindness towards us, we freely abandon our will to punish those have trespassed against us, and we freely employ our will to forgive them.

Let no one suffer as they have made us to suffer. And in so pardoning, O Christ, according to your teaching and example, we commit a revolutionary act against the world principles of retaliation and madness.

We become free from the prison of the Will to Punish, and implore the joyfully approving Father and Son

to send the Holy Spirit

to restore to us all health, to remove the afflictions inflicted upon us, and with the graceful medicine that is God's very self, to restore in us the human health which is the Image of God.

Charles L. Zeiders, Psy.D.

Meditations on Reconciliations

Charles L. Zeiders, Psy.D.

The following meditations on reconciliation are based on the author's lectures given at The Church of the Holy Trinity, Rittenhouse Square, Philadelphia, PA, on 9/24/03 and 2/11/04 as part of that institution's *Trinity Healing Seminars*. Aspects of the spiritual psychology of reconciliation are explored through clinical vignettes, literature, film and stories. Reconciliation is explored and critiqued through the lens of *Christian Holism*, and the God of the Christian revelation is depicted as integral to the holistic healing implicit in the reconciliation process.

From the perspective of *Christian Holism*, Jesus Christ brings everything together. He ultimately unifies us and the universe into a loving, dynamic relationship with the Holy Trinity. He brings everything, including our fragmented minds and ruined friendships, into harmonious interactions. Jesus' death destroys the shattering effect of sin and wonderfully reconnects us to ourselves, creation, and God. A transpersonal insight of staggering psychospiritual implications, this truth was expressed beautifully by St. Paul in Colossians 1:19-20:

> So spacious is he [Christ], so roomy, that everything of God finds its proper place in him without crowding. Not only that, but all the broken and dislocated pieces of the universe, people and things, animals and atoms, get properly fixed and fit together in vibrant harmonies, all because of his death, his blood that was poured down from the cross" (Peterson, 1996, p.422).

So, you have St. Paul with his beautiful vision of Jesus, through his sacrifice, bringing all fragmentation into his fragmented body and causing fragmentation and unreconciliation to die with him on the cross. Then God as Christ surrounds and encases and saturates all things in loving, vibrant interconnectedness.

Jesus Christ is the universal reconciler. Everything comes together in right relationship through Jesus Christ. St. Paul had experiential knowledge of this. Alienated from God, alienated from church, and alienated from himself, Paul lived a destructive life. He participated in the executions of "religious extremists," and he applied himself to destroying communities and people who did not share his worldview. Eventually, however, the resurrected Christ confronted Paul and psychospiritually transformed him. Christ destroyed the sick, fragmented Paul on his cross and resurrected a healthier, whole Paul to a revolutionized, renewed experience of living. As Paul reconciled to God in Christ, he came to see his earlier destructive behavior as intrinsically crazy and outside the healthy life in God with whom he enjoyed intimacy. As he reconciled to God, Paul's subjectivity healed. He experienced himself as living and moving and having his being in God. He found himself reconciled to and saturated with divinity and went on to live among the most generative lives in Christian history.

The Importance of Reconciliation: The Need to Imitate Christ

Jesus Christ reconciled St. Paul and reconciles us to ourselves, to one another, and to God. But Jesus also wants us to participate in his ministry of reconciliation. Jesus is our role model, and he wants us to imitate him. In Matthew 5:23-24, Jesus asks us to reconcile with others with whom we have had a falling out, even before we begin our prayers. Jesus tells us that if our relationships are disordered, we must fix them. Then we can pray.

Jesus taught this, because he knows how things work. He knows that unreconciliation in our relationships will hinder the effectiveness of our prayers—and he wants us to have effective prayers. He does not want our fractured relationships to hinder our deep communication with the Holy Trinity in whom we live and move and have our being.

To reconcile is to bring back into friendship, to harmonize. Reconciliation is a relational movement toward closeness to self, others, and God. An important reason to reconcile is that, if we do not, our unreconciliation will break our hearts. Unreconciliation leaves us with the bitter fruit of alienation and warps our minds. Epidemiological evidence shows that unreconciliation ruins the immune system.[1] It fuels estrangement, and it robs us out of communion with God. Jesus reconciles us to God and wants us to reconcile with one another in order to enjoy the intrinsic health of the reconciled life and have effective communication with the Trinity.

The Parable of the Lost Son

Jesus teaches about reconciliation in the parable of the lost son. (Keep in mind that mine is a psychologist's understanding of the parable, not a theologian's.) Three important players live out the parable's action:

- the father, who owns a big estate,
- a dutiful, older son, who is on task all the time, who keeps himself under parental authority and might even have a type A personality, and
- the younger brother, who wants to do his own thing and does not want to be under parental authority.

Parental authority symbolizes living and moving and having our being in the Trinity.

The younger brother gets his courage up and says to his rich father, "I don't even want to wait until you're dead, Dad; I want my inheritance now. I

An important reason to reconcile is that, if we do not, our unreconciliation will break our hearts. Unreconciliation leaves us with the bitter fruit of alienation and warps our minds.

want to take all that would be mine when you die. I want to take it while you're still living. I want to go away from you. I want to go to a foreign country, and I'll party there." The younger brother's request disrespects the father and hurts his feelings. Because the father loves his son, he is reluctant to acquiesce, but he respects the boy's freedom, so finally he gives him his inheritance. The young man goes to a foreign country, and he lives it up. He engages in "riotous living." He probably buys prostitutes and drinks profusely. Maybe he does drugs as well. His dissolute lifestyle ruins him.

Then a famine hits the land, and a bear market sets in. All economic indicators are down and concurrently the young man runs out of cash. He cannot find a good job and he has no resources for basic necessities. In desperation, the young man gets a job on a pig farm. Down on his luck, he finds himself slopping the hogs and even envying them. He has become a hog butler who serves pigs food that he himself cannot afford. He admits, "I've blown my personal life. Even the hired guys back on Dad's estate have it better than I do here. I've completely ruined my life." So, he brainstorms a solution and concludes, "OK, I could go back to Dad's estate and say, 'Dad, I've sinned against heaven and you. I've done bad things, but I would like you to allow me to return home, no longer as your son, but as a hired hand'."

Why didn't he ask to be reinstated as a son? The younger brother was psychologically astute. He understood human nature enough to know that by rejecting his Dad, he had brought a grotesque relational scenario into force. His selfish behavior interrupted the love between his father and himself. What happens when there is an interruption in love? The rejected person experiences pain, then anger. How do rejected people deal with their anger? They typically seek to punish, humiliate or put into a low status, the people who have broken their hearts. Knowing this, the young man does not presume to come back and say, "Take me back, Dad. Let me be in relationship with you as I was before." He realizes that his father might require him to be humiliated. This is human nature. The son probably resigned himself to the idea that the grotesque relational scenario was even fair. Likely, he concluded, "I hurt Dad, so I deserve to be hurt by Dad in turn.

With this in mind, the lost son starts home, and his father sees him coming from a long way off. Why does his father see him coming from a long way off? Because the father was keeping watch, yearning for his return. He may have thought, "Because I love him, I miss him. Because I miss him, I will welcome him." Upon seeing the boy, the father actually goes out to meet him. Dad literally cannot wait for his son to come home. The son gives his words of apology and—instead of the father saying, "I will now prosecute the grotesque relational scenario and take you back but in a humiliating role,"—he says, "Certainly not! Get in the house. Here's a nice robe." He gives the son good shoes, and he puts a wonderful ring on his finger. He throws a party, and he kills the fatted calf, the best beef in the place. Instead of humiliation time, it's party time. Capable of love, the father bypasses the grotesque relational scenario that weak people perpetrate upon each other— an eye for a eye, a tooth for a tooth. You did that to me, so I'll do this to you. The father was so capable of love that he did not have to play that game. Without complication, he accepted his son back. The requirements of love made everything else superfluous. The father had a beautiful position of strength. Astounded by the loving gift of reconciliation, the son will see that by rejecting his father, he rejected love itself—a love that dwells in his Dad for him and saves him.

In this parable of reconciliation, Jesus tells a final incident: While the party is going on, the responsible older brother is working, and he hears the music. People are dancing, having fun, drinking wine and eating excellent meat. So, he draws near and stands outside the party. He would not go inside, because he begins to think that something is wrong. Asking a servant for information, he learns that his "worthless" younger brother just returned from his disastrous binge and that his Dad rewards the unemployed, destitute, fornicating, miscreant drunk with gifts and a party. The older brother is furious. The father comes out and tries to convince him to join the party. There is plenty for everybody. If the father has enough love for the destitute younger brother, surely he has enough love for the responsible older brother. The older brother does not get the point. He lacks the psychological and spiritual maturity to appreciate how intrinsically reconciling love is—how love can overwhelm the need to hurt those who hurt us. He cannot see how love transcends fairness. The older brother just does not understand. But he is a good guy. We admire him. We appreciate his work ethic. We would probably hire him for a job before we would hire the younger brother, but he is missing something very important. He is starting to think that the father's approach is wrong. He feels cheated because his "worthless" younger brother got a good thing. His weak, wayward younger brother, who injured a relationship, was reconciled back to that relationship by the stronger father who could love.

Jesus ends the parable with a warning to us. We see this older brother really, really upset. He says, "Dad, you're throwing my little brother a party, and you're giving him all kinds of good things. I've been working really, really hard. You won't even kill a goat for me to eat with my friends." The father essentially tells him, "Everything that I have is yours. What's the big deal? Come and enjoy all this good will and harmonious merrymaking." The

He cannot see how love transcends fairness....
Something about reconciliation
heals our fragmented psyches.

older brother struggles to decide whether or not he is going to do it.

If the older brother is not careful, he's going to end up with medical problems. He may brood about how his younger brother should have been punished, and he will get angry and upset. His sympathetic nervous response will activate and will pump out too much adrenaline and cortisol. The older brother will lose neuronal tissue. Anxiety and depression will plague him. His immune system will degrade. He will fail to relate harmoniously to his father and younger brother. His unreconciled, contemptuous stance will generalize into other relationships. He could alienate himself from a lot of blessings. This is a warning to us.

The Alienation of the Unreconciled Mind:
The Case of the Angry Young Man

God wants to reconcile with us, and Jesus Christ teaches us to reconcile with one another. Something about reconciliation heals our fragmented psyches. Yet, our free will plays a huge role in whether or not we enjoy the healing benefits of reconciliation. We can refuse to reconcile—but at a cost.

Here is an example of the alienation of the unreconciled mind: When I started my career in mental health, I worked in an inpatient facility for young adults. A young man in my therapy group was angry at everyone. He seemed to have a special relationship to his anger. His anger came from being rejected and treated cruelly by his parents. He generalized his anger to everyone and lashed out to keep all away. He forgave no one, and he never gave anyone the benefit of the doubt. He was terribly unhappy. He could not be friends with anyone. He could not be vulnerable. He could not experience pleasure, because his body was strangled by the tense muscles of a person ready to fight. He even had a certain aura around his body—as if his anger impregnated the space around him. Sometimes I had the feeling—when he was especially angry—that you could just cook an egg on his head. He was so angry. That is the cost of the unreconciled mind.

To be fair, at the time of his treatment, his parents were probably too dangerous to reconcile with in any practical sense. If the young man, however, could have entered a forgiveness process toward them, he stood a real chance to heal in terms of his anger and underlying rejection wounds. Because healing grace comes to those who forgive, he could have healed internally and reconciled with himself. Also, if he could have accepted the unconditional positive regard of the therapy group—the therapeutic equivalent of love—he might have entered into simultaneously harmonious relations with himself and the group. Reconciliation could have been realized. His defensiveness was understandable, though, because being hurt by others does cause us to distance ourselves from possible future hurt. Wherever he is now, I hope he is well.

The Story of the Actor: A Calamitous Example
of Choosing Self-Contempt over Reconciling Love

We do have a choice about reconciling. We can move toward the people who have hurt us, or we can move toward the people whom we have hurt—and seek to restore the relationship. Both take humility. For some of us, reconciliation with ourselves or others or God is impossible until we experience love. God loves us directly and God loans us love for one another. In many ways, God is always offering us the opportunity to be loved, to be healed, and to be reconciled. We have a choice as to whether we want to accept that love and heal our inner fragments and fractured relationships.

Here is a story of a lost opportunity to accept love, to heal, and to reconcile. An actor who had prided himself on his good looks and ability to sing and dance was down on his luck. Out of work, he sat around his girlfriend's apartment and ate junk food. He got fatter and fatter, and his "six pack" turned to a paunch. Then a director friend called. He said, "Fred, I have a role for you. I want you to perform in my musical." Needing a job, Fred accepted immediately and went back to work—but things were not right. Rehearsing for a dance scene, Fred found he could no longer dance as he once had. He had become uncoordinated. His big stomach made him wobble. He felt ridiculous. He ran from the rehearsal in humiliation and fled to his girlfriend's apartment. Taking off his shirt, he sat on the bed and looked glumly at his big stomach in the mirror. Humiliated, he moaned and groaned so loudly that his girlfriend overheard and rushed into the room. "Fred, what's the matter? You seem really upset."

"I'm just so fat and overweight. I've lost my ability perform. I'm a disgraced whale!" He grabbed his big stomach and squeezed it in anguish. Then his girlfriend reached to him. She tenderly touched his fat shoulder and whispered, "I love you." In that one moment, in her simple gesture, dynamics of reconciliation could have merged with elegance. Fred was fragmented and unreconciled with himself. Fred stood beside himself and could not value himself. But his girlfriend offered him her love and, in so doing, demonstrated to Fred his lovability. By accepting her love, Fred could have healed internally, connected harmoniously to his girlfriend, and experienced God—because to be in love is to be in God. (St. John the Evangelist would say as much.) All Fred had to do was accept her love to begin to heal psychologically, relationally, and spiritually.

What did Fred do? He said, "No!" A perverse sense of pride made him refuse her love. He dashed away—his big fat stomach jiggling. He stormed

He chose fragmentation and estrangement to wholeness and reconciliation. He chose the prideful, isolated prison of self-hatred to the humble freedom of love offered by his girlfriend and God (the wellspring of all love).

into the kitchen, grabbed a donut covered in icing, and feasted on his self-loathing and spite. In this deed, Fred made a choice. He chose fragmentation and estrangement to wholeness and reconciliation. He chose the prideful, isolated prison of self-hatred to the humble freedom of love offered by his girlfriend and God (the wellspring of all love).

The Reconciliation of Jean Valjean: Acceptance of a Bishop's Love Heals Jean Valjean Internally, Relationally, and Spiritually

Reconciliation is offered to us by God in love, and by people, who often act unconsciously as God's ambassadors. Sometimes, for reasons of false pride or defensiveness, we reject it and fail to heal. At other times, in the mystery of grace, we apprehend the divine father offering relationship (often through others or circumstances), and in the blinking of an eye, we experience the transformative nature of reconciliation with self, others, and the Trinity.

Victor Hugo's novel *Les Misérables* illustrates this transpersonal phenomenon. There's one scene that's absolutely astounding. It holds true both psychologically and spiritually. Jean Valjean is on the run. Convicted of a crime, he has just exited a physical prison, but he can neither escape nor gain parole from his metaphysical prison. More animal than man, he has suffered inhuman treatment by the prison authorities. Injured from cruelties, he has no reason to love himself or anyone, let alone to seek God or to entertain ideas of reconciliation. This man is purely in survival mode, trudging from village to village, trying to avoid the authorities, and impossibly trying to put prison behind him, even as he carries it in his heart. Jean Valjean finally ends up in the house of a bishop. Desperate for food and shelter, Valjean begs the bishop's hospitality, and—offending Jean's cynicism—the bishop graciously invites Valjean to enjoy his hospitality. Graciousness is foreign to the convict, and he cannot trust it. But, in his neediness, he eats the food and drinks the wine the bishop offers him, and he accepts the holy man's offer for shelter from the night.

Then, while the bishop is sleeping, Jean Valjean rises from his bed, steals most of the bishop's silver—including cutlery and religious items—throws them into a sack, dashes from the house, and flees into the night. In the morning, the bishop awakens to find his silver, save for two priceless candlesticks, has been stolen. The bishop is deeply hurt and disappointed. Jean Valjean, meanwhile is on the run; he looks extraordinarily fugitive, and the gendarmes easily spot him. When the gendarmes grab him, they recognize the engravings on the silver, and they bring Jean Valjean and the silver back to the house of the bishop. The gendarmes present the stolen silver and Jean Valjean to the bishop. They say, "We have found this criminal, this rogue with your silver. We want to return it, and then we are going to throw this wretch back into prison." But the bishop is like the father in Jesus' parable of the lost son. Valjean expects punishment. He is ignorant to the fact that love enables the bishop to transcend justice. To the gendarmes' remarks, the bishop replies "Oh, no, gentleman. You are mistaken. This man has been my guest, and he is a friend of mine. He has not stolen my silver. It is a gift I have given to him. But you have brought him back, and I am pleased. Now I can give him these candlesticks as well." Satisfied, the gendarmes leave, and the bishop gifts Jean Valjean with the very candlesticks the criminal forgot to steal. Instantaneously, Jean Valjean experiences the healing agony of accepted love. He realizes that despite his criminal behavior towards this holy man, this man can love him. Experiencing his lovability through the bishop, he accepts that love into his fragmented soul. The love he accepts is a medicine that reconciles him to himself in terms of psychological healing, to the bishop in terms of relational healing, and to God in terms of spiritual healing. Overwhelmed, he weeps in the relief that comes from the healing remedy of the love that reconciles.

The actor in the previous story rejected love and lost the opportunity to heal and reconcile. In Victor Hugo's story, Jean Valjean's acceptance of love is the act of will that unleashes psychological connectedness and spiritual transformation. Willing acceptance of offered love (human or divine) is a key component to *Christian Holism*'s appreciation of reconciliation.

Going Straight to Reconciliation:
Exploring the Christian Unconscious of a David Lynch Film

Film director David Lynch shot a film entitled *The Straight Story*. It's based on a true story about a man named Alvin Straight, who lived in Middle America. Poor and elderly, Alvin Straight suffered bad health. He walked with two canes, and, after an eye exam revealed Alvin's deteriorated eyesight, his doctor revoked his driver's license. Crippled and forbidden to drive, Alvin felt terrible. Then, he received more bad news. Alvin's brother, Lyle, who lived three hundred miles away, had just had a stroke and was expected to die soon. Alvin Straight became very concerned. Many years ago, Alvin and Lyle were drinking heavily, and they started to argue. They said drunken words that were infuriating and caused disharmony between them. Since that night of intoxication and acrimonious exchange, the two brothers had become estranged. But when poor health confronted Alvin with his and Lyle's mortality, he realized that time was running out. He remembered how

Willing acceptance of offered love (human or divine) is a key component to *Christian Holism's* appreciation of reconciliation.

much he loved Lyle, and he was humbled to admit that he could not recall the specifics of the point of disagreement between them. Realizing the pointlessness of their estrangement, he felt tremendous pressure to go straight to Lyle to restore the harmony of the relationship. But he could no longer drive a car, and public transportation came nowhere near Lyle's cabin. So, single-minded and resolved, Alvin bought a broken-down, second-hand *John Deer* lawn mower tractor. The crippled, half blind man forced his broken body behind the wheel and started the three hundred mile trek, riding on the shoulder of the road, to reconcile with Lyle before he died.

Clinical experience has demonstrated to me that the Holy Spirit affiliates with and works through people who follow the teachings of Jesus Christ—even if that following is informal or unconscious. From the perspective of *Christian Holism*, this spiritual dynamic is especially important to understanding some of the ministerial adventures that confronted Alvin as he pilgrimaged toward Lyle. Alvin responded affirmatively to the pressure of his conscience and the gentle prompting of the Holy Spirit to reconcile with Lyle. Then, opportunities synchronously opened for Alvin Straight to become a minister of reconciliation. The Holy Spirit recognized in Alvin a kindred spirit and affiliated with him—making him capable of advancing the interests of God.

Here is one example. Early in Alvin's pilgrimage of reconciliation, he sat by his campfire one evening, when a pregnant teenage girl walked into his campsite. Angry and scared, she had run away from her family. She confided in Alvin, "I'm running away from home. My parents hate me. I hate them. They don't understand me. If they find out about the pregnancy, they'll kill me, etc."

Alvin Straight listened to her talk; then he said, "I want to tell you something. I'm old now, and you probably can't imagine me as a Dad, but when I was a young man, I had lots of kids, and I used to play a game with them. I'd grab a stick and give it to my kids and have them try to break it. They would break the stick over their knees and of, course, the stick would just snap in two. To break one stick is easy. Then I'd have the kids gather a bunch of sticks and wrap them in a bundle with a rope. I'd have them try to break the bundled sticks. But bundled sticks are strong, and they couldn't break the bundle. I'd tell the kids that alone we're like the single stick, alone we break pretty easy. But all the sticks together, that's our family. Together we're not likely to break, because we make each other strong." Finished with his story, Alvin fell asleep. The next morning, the girl was gone. By the campfire, she had left a bundle of sticks tied together with a rope. In this way, she communicated that she had understood Alvin's (and ultimately God's) point. She was going home to try to work things out with her family. In reconciliation was her strength.

Alvin had other chances to be a minister of reconciliation. At one point in his journey, his lawnmower broke down. He found two brothers who were mechanics to repair his lawnmower. These brothers were the best lawnmower repairmen in the town, but they bickered incessantly. Alvin Straight observed these brothers humiliate one another. He watched them butcher each other's self-esteem, and publicly rob each other of dignity. He witnessed the kind of behavior that destroys love. Then, in a kind way, he said, "Boys, I appreciate the fact that you have repaired my lawnmower, because I need it to get to my brother Lyle. The whole reason that a broken down old man like me is riding a broken down old lawnmower like that is because I didn't realize that the most important thing in the world is the love of a brother. Boys, when I was your age, I wish I would have known how important my brother Lyle was. I wish I would have treated him with the utmost respect, rather than the meanness with which I did. Now I have to repair me and Lyle, just like you boys repaired my tractor. I just thought you boys ought to know that." Dumbstruck the brothers gaped at each other. Their relationally ruinous behavior had been exposed. They realized that they needed to repent of their pointless fighting in order to reconcile and preserve their intrinsically valuable relationship. Alvin Straight had set them straight. The brothers got the point.

The experience of Alvin Straight illustrates a truth about the Christian psychospirituality of reconciliation. God not only reconciles with us through Christ, but God also privileges us to represent the Kingdom of Heaven to offer reconciliation to the world. When we respond to God or godly conciliatory impulses, we become entrained by God to participate in the Holy Trinity's ministry of reconciliation. St. Paul writes that "We are therefore Christ's ambassadors, as though God were making his appeal [for reconciliation] through us" (2 Cor. 5:20, NIV, 1985, p. 1769). When Alvin Straight decided that he was going to reconcile with Lyle, he became God's ambassador of reconciliation. The divine principle poured out of him into the lives of the pregnant girl and the brothers, as though God were making his appeal to them through Alvin Straight. Because Alvin responded to the godly impulse to reconcile, the psyches and relationships of others were blessed and healed.

At the end of his journey. Alvin found Lyle. He parked his old lawn mower in front of Lyle's cabin. He yelled for Lyle, and from inside the cabin Lyle yelled for him. They shuffled toward each other and sat upon chairs on Lyle's dilapidated porch. The two brothers engaged in no relational processing—no working through or negotiations. They simply sat together as the invisible God undid their estrangement and reconciled them.

God not only reconciles with us through Christ, but God also privileges us to represent the Kingdom of Heaven to offer reconciliation to the world.

The Old Lady and the Girl: A Pilgrimage from Teasing to Togetherness

Here is another story of reconciliation about an old lady who lived in a southern town. Her family had moved away or died, and she had no friends. She was quite lonely. For some reason, nobody reached out to her, and, like a lot of society's throw-aways, she became demoralized, took less care of herself, and developed a reputation for being a bit odd. One day, tired of just cats for company, she went for a walk and came across a gaggle of seven seventh grade girls. The thirteen-year-olds knew that the woman had a reputation for being a little peculiar, and, due to their parents' role-modeling of ostracizing the old lady, they felt comfortable teasing her. The leader of the gaggle of girls engaged the old lady in conversation. In a mocking way that amused her friends but was lost on the contact starved old lady, the girl chatted her up with cruel affability and politeness. Her friends tittered, but the old lady did not notice. So happy to have contact with someone other than her cats, she responded to the disingenuous overtures of the lead girl, and tried to engage all the girls, asking them their names and interests, etc. The girls were having a great time at the old lady's expense. Making sport of the old lady with false deference and exaggerated good manners, they tittered to themselves and gave each other knowing glances. But the poor woman became excited and happy. She mistook the girls' interest as genuine and invited them to her home. "Why don't you come to my house today after school? I'll buy treats. I have this wonderful collection of dolls. We can have a tea party together. I can show you the dolls, and if you want to, you can play with them." Teasing the old lady, the girls replied, "Certainly, we'll be there. We'll be happy to come to your party and play with your dolls." Then, they ran off to school. They laughed among themselves and continued to make sport of the old woman, and to congratulate one another at tricking her. None of the girls intended to really honor the old lady's invitation, but the old lady did not know this. Enthusiastically, she went out and bought all sorts of wonderful things for the tea party. Years had gone by since she had entertained. She felt so happy that she was almost confused. She set up her table. She put a white cloth on it and took her precious silver and china from the storage boxes. She set seven places and breathlessly waited for her young guests. Amid the sound of her old clock ticking, she sat and sat and, she waited quietly into the evening. As evening came, she felt the ache of rejection and realized that the girls were just teasing her. They did not really like her, and they would not come. With this realization, she went to bed and slept in the sorrow of rejection.

There was one little girl in the gaggle of seventh graders who knew right from wrong. She went along with the gag, but she knew that she and the other girls had trespassed against the old lady. That night she slept poorly. Visions of the old lady sitting in sorrow kept waking her. Her heart went out to the old lady, and, in her compassion, she wanted to make things right. But she also felt afraid. If she approached the old lady with an apology, the old lady might be furious. She might yell at the girl or guilt-trip her. But summoning her courage, the girl decided to apologize. After school, she went straight to the old lady's house and knocked. The old lady opened the door and stared at the girl. All day long, the girl had rehearsed her apology, and, as she offered it, she trembled. "I'm sorry my friends and I did not come to your party as we said we would, ma'am. We were mean to inconvenience you, and I'm sorry we did." The old woman was silent, and the girl read anger and pain on her face. The girl felt afraid until something like love shone through the old lady's expression. The old lady smiled and invited the girl inside. "I still have some treats left over from yesterday." The girl followed her to the kitchen, and the old lady set out treats, and they ate and drank together. As they conversed, they began to have fun and discovered that they liked each other. When the girl finally left, it was evening. She left with a doll that the old lady had given to her as a present. The girl came back to visit the old lady again and again. For the remainder of the old lady's life they were friends and enjoyed a rare closeness.

This is a wonderful example of the girl being the prodigal son, and the little old lady being the father. The girl's behavior also reiterates Alvin Straight's role modeling of going straight to the person with whom one has to reconcile and not going on a lot of detours. The hurt old lady invited her in and both of them were healed of their sin-induced internal and relational fragmentation. *Christian Holism* finds that at the heart of such reconciliation is love, and this love is our revealed God.

A Slob of Paradise who Reconciled with his Denigrating Dad

A good friend of mine has given me permission to share his story. My friend calls himself "A Slob of Paradise" because he sees himself as a fallen man with a lots of rough edges—although he is deeply committed to Jesus Christ. We met in the tenth grade. In those days, he was high strung, shy, and oddly gifted at delinquency. His father played a big role in his issues. A survivor of staggering rural poverty, his father was angry, bitter, and insecure. He was threatened by his son's gifts and scapegoated him for his own unhappiness. Nothing the young man did could please his father. My friend grew up with his dad unavailable to him as a mentor or a coach. Compulsively, he tried to please his father, but his father always found fault with him.

After we graduated from high school, my friend moved into an apartment

As they conversed, they began to have fun and discovered that they liked each other .... The girl came back to visit the old lady again and again. For the remainder of the old lady's life they were friends and enjoyed a rare closeness.

near South Street in Philadelphia. At a local bar, he met a pretty girl and tried to flirt with her, but she said, "Look, it's just not gonna work, because I have to get up for church tomorrow, but you can meet me at the Presbyterian Church at Eighth & Pine streets." Getting a date with her would be an interesting challenge, so he went to her church to ask her out, but she ignored him. Yet, he felt that the service was fantastic. It was the perfect service for a young man who had real issues with authority. A missionary from the Sanctuary Movement gave the sermon. In the 1980s, the Sanctuary Movement consisted of radical young Christians who smuggled refugees and dissidents out of El Salvador and Guatemala. The Sanctuary Christians protected political and economic reformers who were death-listed by the Central American oligarchs. My friend heard this Sanctuary missionary speaking, and he was absolutely radicalized. He moved to Tucson, Arizona and joined the movement. He learned Spanish, and, at great peril to himself, smuggled Christians fleeing a well-founded fear of persecution out of Central America to the Mexican border. From there, he would secretly cross the dissidents into the United States, risking a five year Federal prison sentence for each person he smuggled. It was a very successful ministry, and he saved many Christian lives. He was arrested several times, but the charges were dropped, presumably because the government feared a public reaction to the sentencing of Christians for saving other Christians from persecution.

Periodically, during those dangerous years in the Sanctuary Movement, my friend would go on furlough. He would visit his Dad hoping that his father would finally approve of him. He hoped that his father would recognize his intelligence for learning Spanish, his commitment to Christian service, and his courage to risk imprisonment. He hoped that his father would recognize that Central American Christians were alive and in Sanctuary in North America because of his ministry and the risks he took. But his Dad continued as before and always put him down. His father refused to see this man for the good, brave man that he was. With irrational negativity, he continued faulting and criticizing his son. Then, one day my friend decided that he could not allow his father to trespass against him anymore. He thought, "I have to take responsibility for good stewardship over my own well-being, my own psychology, my own soul. Like the people I have saved, I am made in the Image of God. I cannot put myself in harm's way anymore. If my father is going to perpetuate this cruelty against me, I have to take responsibility for preventing it. That could mean cutting off relations, but my first choice is reconciliation—if my father will treat me appropriately." So, he made a special visit to his father. He was frightened and, characteristically, his father started criticizing him—not about anything remarkable, but giving and receiving denigration was just the way their dysfunctional relationship worked. This time, though, my friend said, "Dad, you just can't do this. This is all you do. This is all we do. I come here, and I'm your victim. You relate to me in this surreal and very cruel way. It's unworthy of you, and it's unworthy of me." Then, of course, in a fury the old man interrupted and redoubled putting-down his son to hobble this threatening communication. But his son said, "No, Dad, that's our old way of relating. If you want to relate to me in this sadistic way, it's not gonna happen, because I am not your victim anymore. Now, I don't know exactly what messed you up so much and why you take it out on me. But I am willing to let the past, and what a bad Dad you've been, wash away. But you have to knock it off, or I'll go, and you won't see me again, because I have to protect myself from your put downs." To the father's credit, he heard his son. He wiped a tear from his eye, and the two of them started to reconcile at that very moment. It was difficult but both men entered into a commitment of repair, respect, and reconciliation. Today the father acknowledges that his son is an accomplished international missionary—as well as a very personal missionary to him. The son courageously risked their relationship in order to transform it from sadomasochism to genuine love.

Recently, I attended my friend's wedding, and it was beautiful to see him and his father with their arms around each other. They smiled at each other a lot and seemed to enjoy genuine affection in their relationship. In following Christ, there is risk, but genuine reconciliation is really achievable.

Clearing Mistaken Assumptions about the Other
to Foster Reconciliation: The Madness of Mind-Reading

In my consulting practice, I find that people sometimes entertain skewed assumptions about one another's motivation and behavior. They read motivations into another's behavior which are simply untrue. This leads to misunderstandings that cause profound estrangement. Once these misapprehensions are made conscious, however, reconciliation can occur in light of the truth.

I had an interesting consult, for example, with a group of metallurgical engineers. A real problem existed between two of the leaders: the top executive and his talented chief scientist. Shortly after the executive hired the chief scientist, their relationship deteriorated from initial cordiality to malignant acrimony. They argued so much and communicated so poorly that business began to suffer. So they invited me to consult with them, and, in the course of my data gathering, I learned that the chief scientist's past relation-

The son courageously risked their relationship in order to transform it from sadomasochism to genuine love.

ship with her father played a decisive role in her current difficulties with the top executive. Her father had been ragingly alcoholic and ragingly abusive, causing his brilliant daughter to grow into a woman with a father-shaped gap in her heart. She married someone like her Dad, hoping that he would support and endorse her, but he abandoned her to his own preference for drink. She divorced him and remained lonely but was superior in her profession. The top executive of the metallurgical firm recognized her gifts and hired her. Observing her high level of performance, he said to himself, "She's a wonderful scientist and manger and knows how to drive projects forward. The last thing I want to do is offend her by micromanaging her." Respecting his chief scientist's competence, the top executive managed her with a hands-off style, as a sign of respect. But the chief scientist experienced this as abandonment and read the abusive neglect of her ex-husband and father into the top executive's managerial absence. The way these two people were missing one another was almost Shakespearean. She needed affirmation, but he did not want to offend her by getting into her part of the business. Once their assumptions were made conscious, they were able to work together and become colleagues and friends.

As a cognitive-behaviorist, I find that much reconciliation can occur when estranged parties discuss their assumptions about each other. Often, one party believes they know what motivates another party but are mistaken. This "mind reading error" can estrange husbands and wives. In one case, the husband was disgruntled with his wife for over a year. He entertained the assumption that she knew the exact nature of his needs but simply refused to meet them. This interpretation of her behavior left him feeling rejected and angry. During therapy, his wife was surprised that he complained of so many unmet needs. When she asked, "Why didn't you tell me you needed me to do those things?", he replied, "I thought you knew I needed them." The wife rightly pointed out that she could not read his mind and should not be held responsible for failing to meet needs about which she did not know. Healing of the relationship involved the husband abandoning the assumption that his wife could read his mind. He took responsibility for telling her what his needs were. Once the wife had the information, she was able to meet those needs, and the couple fell in love again. Clearing away his erroneous assumption was the beginning of their reconciliation.

Not Choosing or Choosing Reconciliation with God through Christ: The Example of Faustus and an Anti-Faustus

Because God wants to reconcile with us, he designed the sacrifice of Jesus Christ to clear away the debris of sin that alienates us from a loving, dynamic relationship with him. God loves us so much we can repeatedly offer our sins (Even the big ones!) to Christ's sacrifice and conclude our disastrous alienation from the loving Trinity. Yet, God respects our freedom. We can choose to reject Christ's sacrifice and God's desire for no-fault reconciliation. We can remain in hellish alienation—at a cost. This negative psychospirituality has been explored in a play by Christopher Marlowe (a contemporary of Shakespeare's), who wrote a play entitled Dr. Faustus.

A brilliant scholar, theologian and scientist, Faustus taught at a big university in medieval Germany. After reading many, many books, he suffered from boredom, restlessness, and low grade depression. He did not love anyone, nor did he seem to like himself. Faustus cultivated morose thoughts and focused on how terrible he felt. He refused to get involved in prayer, spiritual direction, or spiritually therapeutic disciplines that might have helped. Instead, he closed himself in his office and engaged in weird reflections. He mused, "I would sell my soul to the devil in order to get some glamorous, occult knowledge to spice up my life." Mephistopheles, a henchman of Satan showed up and said, "I heard that. We can definitely work out a deal. Here's the contract: we'll give you all the occult knowledge that you want. You'll be able to have spells and supernatural, forbidden powers that every wizard in Europe will envy. In return, at the end of a period of years, we will get your soul for eternity. Is it a deal?" Faustus exclaimed, "Where do I sign?" Faustus the moron! He signed the contract with Mephistopheles and received the forbidden, occult powers. Faustus then ravaged Europe, sabotaged the church, and pursued interesting, useless knowledge through conversations with devils. Suddenly, at the end of the contract period, Faustus realized that he had made a terrible mistake. On the eve on which Mephistopheles and other devils were to claim his soul and drag it into hell, Faustus wrung his hands in his office. He said to himself, "Even now one drop of Christ's blood could save me!" Then, in the next instant, he could not bring himself to throw himself on the mercy of God. He just could not do it. There was some flaw in the employment of his free will.

Marlowe, in his depiction of Faustus, neglected to depict what happened in the scholar's developmental and learning history that compromised his character so much. But the fact is, Faustus refused to avail himself of that salvational drop of Christ's blood. In the image of Christ's blood, God showed Faustus that Jesus was literally dying to destroy the sin that estranged Faustus from the Trinity. In that image of shed blood, God said to Faustus, "Forget the occult stuff and dealing with the devil, the false gods, your narcissism, whatever. Give all the bad stuff and the consequences to

As a cognitive-behaviorist, I find that much reconciliation can occur when estranged parties discuss their assumptions about each other. Often, one party believes they know what motivates another party but are mistaken. This "mind reading error" can estrange ....

me. I'll pay the price. Just come back! On my cross I'm dying to reconnect with you!" But Faustus was unwilling to allow Christ's blood to accomplish this reconciliation. Instead, he chose hell. In a horrible, bloody scene, the devils came, and they dragged him to perdition. The next morning, upon entering his study, his university colleagues found the smoking remains of Faustus' academic robes. That was all that was left. Something went wrong with Faustus' choosing. God offered Faustus reconciliation, but something perverse in the scholar's nature caused him to choose the torment of estrangement. Faustus' story is a cautionary tale.

When we think about reconciliation with God, however, we should be optimistic. *Christian Holism* embraces the good news of the Christian revelation—which is that God came into the world to save us from our mistakes and to delight with us in this world and the next. A charming medieval story about the final mortal moments of an old sinner illustrates this transpersonal reality:

The Devil and the Dying Man

It is said that the devil came once to a dying man. He held in his hand a long parchment roll in which was set down all the man's sins from birth to the passing hour; all the idle words he had spoken, all the falsehoods he had told, all the impure and profane words he had uttered, all his angry words, all his wanton words, all his scandals, all his omissions. Next came his thoughts; and then his acts of sin, arrayed under the ten commandments. It was a frightful listing indeed. Then Satan said, "What have you as a set-off against this list of sins?" The sick man replied, "Put this down first: 'The blood of Christ cleanseth from all sin;' and underneath add this: 'Whosoever believeth in Me shall not perish, but have everlasting life'." Whereupon the devil vanished; and the sick man died with these words on his lips, 'Whosoever shall lay anything to the charge of God's elect? It is God that justifieth. Who is he that condemneth?" (Brewer, 1992, p. 212)

The hero of this little story is an anti-Faustus, a man who uses his free will wisely. He chooses to evade the hell of estrangement from God by assenting to let the shed blood of Christ destroy the alienating effects of his mistakes. His choice leads to reconciliation with God: a reconciliation which Jesus images for us in the form of a party in heaven (Lk. 15)—a transcendent enjoyment of dynamic harmony with the Trinity and our loved selves. Wonderfully, we can choose such reconciliation.

Reference Note

1.   For an excellent discussion of this point read Ornish (1998).

References

Brewer, E. (1992). *A dictionary of miracles.* Philadelphia, PA: J.B. Lippincott Co.

Ornish, D. (1998). *Love and survival: 8 pathways to intimacy and health.* New York: HarperPerrenial.

Peterson, E. (1996). *The message.* Colorado Springs, CO: NavPress Publishing Group

Dreams and *Christian Holism*: Therapy and the Nocturnal Voice of God*

Charles L. Zeiders, Psy.D.

This article develops the theory and practice of clinical dream work within the context of *Christian Holism*. *Christian Holism* articulates the idea that the Holy Spirit is clinically present and active during clinical work, and therefore plays a mysterious but real part in the unfolding of dream meanings. It is argued that dreams have played a positive part in human experience in Old and New Testament times and during formative epochs within Christian History. The point is made that insights from depth psychology and dream physiology are useful to practitioners of *Christian Holism*, in that such knowledge is engraced as the practitioner offers this knowledge base to God for the client's healing.

T o dream is to hear the voice of God within the soul. During Rapid Eye Movement (REM) sleep the body and mind experience exquisite changes—an internal liturgy—that inaugurate the entrance of internal, meaningful visions. When invited, God enlightens the dreamer's mind to understand dreams in ways that are beautiful, coherent, and healing. God's Holy Spirit shows the dreamer the meaning of the dream, and God inspires the dreamer to know what good action he or she must take to do well. In the context of psychotherapy, God works to bless both client and clinician with dream interpretations that lead to Holism—a state of dynamic unity with self, others, creation, and the Trinity. At all times God wants us to do well, and dreams are avenues through which God blesses us. From within the divine imagination, God created dream processes so that we might thrive in all the ways that God seeks for us to enjoy. The good psychotherapy of dream work is founded in the Christian experience of holy dreams recorded in scripture, positive appreciation of dreams by the Church fathers, and positive encounters with God's blessings through dreams among contemporary believers. Finally, the goodness that comes into the lives of clients, when the Holy Spirit is invited to bless the dream work in the name of Christ, speaks to the value of dream work in the context of clinical psychology and *Chris-*

* A large portion of this article was first published in *The Journal of Christian Healing*, Volume 22, #3&4, Fall/Winter, 2001, pp. 58-71.

tian Holism. I want to show that scripture and church tradition are favorable to dreams. I then discuss *Christian Holism*'s dream stance and offer cases that illustrate the healing value of dream work when the clinical situation employs faith that the Holy Spirit is lovingly involved in the dream and its interpretation.

Dreams in Scripture

Historically, God employs dreams, dream-like experiences, and dream interpretation to help his people. In Genesis, via a dream, God established a covenant with Abraham, promising descendants, land, and protection (Gen. 15:12-16). God renewed this covenant with Jacob during Jacob's famous ladder dream (Gen. 28:11-16). Joseph, whose future a divine dream foretold (Gen. 37), influenced Pharaoh through dream interpretation and reached the rank of viceroy, eventually bringing the Jews to Egypt. Advising the King of Babylon, Daniel interpreted Nebuchadnezzar's dreams, because God graced him with "the gift of interpreting every kind of vision and dream" (Dan. 1:17). Daniel referred to God as The Revealer of Mysteries who provides dreams so that dreamers might understand their inmost thoughts (Dan. 2:30).

In the New Testament, dreams are instrumental in the birth and protection of the child Jesus. An angel appears to Joseph in a dream, advising him not to divorce Mary, because she has conceived her child by the Holy Spirit (Mt. 1:20-21). A dream warns the Magi not to report to murderous Herod the location of the infant Christ (Mt. 2:12). A dream warns Joseph to avoid the Massacre of the Innocents by escaping with the holy family into Egypt (Mt. 2:13). A dream commands Joseph to return the Holy Family to Israel upon Herod's death (Mt. 2:20)

Important events in the lives of St. Peter and St. Paul occur in dream-like visions. In a trance, Peter receives God's declaration that all foods are clean, freeing Peter to eat with Gentiles and evangelize them as equals (Acts 10:16). In a night vision, Paul saw a man who begged, "Come over to Macedonia and help us" (Acts 16:9), inspiring Paul to immediately depart on a missionary journey. These examples show that God's will can often be gleaned from dreams and dream-like experiences.

Dreams in the Early Church

Some Church fathers thought highly of dreams, others did not. Emphasizing the Church fathers' positive disposition toward dreams in the first five centuries, Savary, Berne, and Williams (1984) write,

> According to John Chrysostom, dreams are enough for God to send to those who are attuned to God, since they do not need vision or other more startling divine revelations.
> Tertullian ... spoke of dreams as one of the *charismata* of God, and

The good psychotherapy of dream work is founded in the Christian experience of holy dreams recorded in scripture, positive appreciation of dreams by the Church fathers, and positive encounters with God's blessings through dreams among contemporary believers.

believed that dreams and visions were promised to people of his own day just as much as they were to the first apostles. Origin ... saw dreams as part of God's providence "for the benefit of the one who had the dream and for those who hear the account of it from him."

Cyprion, bishop of Carthage in 250 A.D., one of the father's of the Latin Church, asserted that the very councils of the Church were guided by God through dreams and "many and manifests visions." And in Gregory of Nazianzen's Church in Constantinople, according to Church historian Sozomen, "the power of God was there manifested, and was helpful both in waking visions and in dreams, often for the re-lief of many diseases and for those afflicted by some sudden crisis in their affairs."

Bishop Cyprian of Carthage wrote so much of his direct encounters with God in dreams and visions that twentieth century editors of his writing felt a need to apologize for them. Gregory Thaumaturgus, origi-nally a student of Roman law, was led to the Christian faith in a beauti-ful dream that involved John the Evangelist and Mary, the Mother of Jesus. Dionysius ... received confirmation in a dream to study both pa-gan and heretical Christian writings: the voice in the dream assured him he need fear nothing because his faith was secure. Constantine, re-ceived an important dream-vision before his battle for Rome, which eventually opened up a new era of Western civilization.

"Dreams, more than any other thing, entice us toward hope," wrote Synesius of Cyrene, a fifth century Bishop of Ptolemais. "And when our heart spontaneously presents hope to us, as happens in our sleeping state, then we have in the promise of our dreams a pledge from the di-vinity (p. 39).

The Church fathers thought highly of dreams, because Christians experi-enced God's grace through them. However, some Church father's hesitated to become dream enthusiasts. They felt, because of the reality of evil, and the fallen aspect of human nature, that dreams needed to be judiciously con-sidered.

While acknowledging that God could be experienced in dreams, [some Fathers] were also careful to note that dreams are often no more than the eruption of irrational emotions into one's sleeping consciousness. Gregory of Nyssa, for instance, asserted that many dreams reflect the animal side of our nature, the offspring of the passions of anger and desire—a view not far from Sigmund Freud's. He also noted a more mundane class of dreams that arise from traces of memory of our daily routines. Thus, the early Christian view of the significance of dreams can be described as generally balanced (Lewis, 1995, p. 47).

While valuing dreams, the early church did not overvalue dreams. Acknowledging that aspects of the fallen nature can come through dreams, early Christians also found God speaking through them. The following apocryphal dream exemplifies the early church's appreciation of the need to discern if God is working through the dream, and then the importance of acting on that information. In this example, the Emperor Constantine dreams of the innocence of three officers condemned for treason.

> *Three officers ... being falsely accused to Constantine were condemned to death. At night, St. Nicholas appeared to the emperor and his judge Ablavius and said to them, "Those three men are innocent; and, unless they are released in the morning, war shall desolate the land, and thou and all thine shall perish by the sword. I, Nicholas of Myra, forewarn you." When the emperor and judge met the next morning, they conferred together of the vision and caused the three officers to be brought before them. "Tell me," said the emperor, "have any of you three any skill in necromancy?" They answered, "No." The emperor then sent them to St. Nicholas with a present consisting of the four Gospels in letters of gold, and a gold thurible; and charged them with this message, "The emperor begs St. Nicholas not to threaten him, but to pray for him. (Brewer, 1992, p.119).*

Importantly, this ancient story suggests that Constantine (and his judge Ablavius who co-dreampt of St. Nicholas' admonition) took it for granted that dreams can convey important information about what God desires. Before treating the dream as utterly reliable, however, Constantine first discerned that the dream originated from no fallen source. Ruling out sorcery as the dream's origin, Constantine then could act upon the dream decisively. He released the innocent officers and asked St. Nicholas to intercede to clear the realm of the sin of injustice, and to restore God's favor to the empire. The dream provided Constantine with an impetus to avoid injustice and seek God's grace and was useful to him following discernment.

In the middle ages, some dreams were considered special signifiers of the divine will. The following important and holy dream, for example, includes the night vision of Bishop Bruno (1002-1054), who later became Pope Leo IX.

One day Bruno, Bishop of Toul, saw in his dream a deformed old woman, who haunted him with great persistency, and treated him with great familiarity. She was hideously ugly, clothed in filthy rags, her hair disheveled, and altogether one could scarcely recognize in her the human form. Disgusted with her general appearance, the bishop tried to avoid her; but the more he shrank from her, the more she clung to him. Annoyed by this importunity, Bruno made the sign of the cross; whereupon she fell to the earth as dead, and rose up again lovely as an angel. While pondering on the meaning of this vision, the abbot Odilo, lately dead, came before him, and said, "Happy man, you have delivered her soul from death." Wilbert, the biographer of our saint, and his contemporary, informs us that the old woman represented the Church, which at the time was in a most deplorable state, but Bruno in his pontificate was employed by God to restore it to its original beauty (Brewer, 1992, p. 119).

Allegorical and prophetic, this God-given dream shows Bruno that the church had entered a fallen state so personally revolting to him as to tempt him to escape facing the ugliness of the Church's problems. Next, he allowed his exasperation—with God's help—to propel him from escapism to action. As pope, he would commit spiritual and ecclesiastical deeds that would resurrect the church from the ugliness of her spiritual death. The dream used glorified (and thus spiritually credible) Abbot Odilo as a holy mouth-piece to exhort Bruno to assume a successful, restorative pontificate. In symbolic language, the dream charged and encouraged this pope to heal the church of her ugly spiritual ailments and restore her to the ever-beautiful life of grace. It also predicted his success.

God used dreams in both Testaments, the early church, and during the middle ages. God continues to speak to the church through dreams, and practitioners of *Christian Holism* address dreams directly.

Dreams and *Christian Holism*

Christian Holism views dreams as a manifestation of grace. Just as God graces our incarnated state with beating hearts and breathing lungs to bless our bodies with health, God naturally graces our sleeping minds with dreams to similarly bless our souls with health. We dream true things about ourselves, reflect on right and wrong, discover the subjective and objective future, uncover keys to psychological healing, and find our thoughts guided by good metaphors. All of this represents God's grace acting in the natural dream machinery of our souls. *Christian Holism* also finds grace contained

... Christian Holism begins dream interpretation by explicitly asking God the Father to send the Holy Spirit in the name of Jesus Christ to take charge of the clinical situation and to assist the therapist and the patient in their consultation.

in social science, through which psychologists continue to discover true, useful methods to understand the content of dreams. Psychoanalysts,[1] analytical psychologists, and research physiologists all advance truth about the way God naturally blesses our dreaming minds and how the content of our dreams might be beneficial to us. In *Christian Holism*, dream interpretation draws upon the truth and utility contained in psychological methods to understand the grace inherent in dreams. Yet *Christian Holism* does not look initially to dream content nor to specific psychological interpretive methods to find benefit for patients. While natural grace shines through creation, the Fall subverts that grace. For this reason, *Christian Holism* begins dream interpretation by explicitly asking God the Father to send the Holy Spirit in the name of Jesus Christ to take charge of the clinical situation and to assist the therapist and the patient in their consultation. *Christian Holism* places dream content and all psychological interpretive methods at the disposal of the Spirit. If the dream is valuable to God's purpose, it is believed that the Holy Spirit will provide discernment and guidance. This is true even of dreams that are quite disturbing.

> ... [E]verything in the universe is God's, [and] all dreams somehow reflect God's purposes and plans for our lives. Even the most demonic or terrifying presences in dreams can be worked with and their energy transformed. Dreams ... present us with what we really need to deal with to fulfill God's need and purpose for our lives (Savary, Berne, & Williams, 1984, p. 41).

The Spirit perfectly knows the dream's meaning and the best interpretive method,[2] whether social scientific or word of knowledge. Therapy enters a state of supernatural grace and the integrity of the dream interpretation is enhanced. Importantly, the Spirit can make even the nightmare redemptive.

What follows are clinical situations involving dreams and dream interpretations addressed in the Spirit of *Christian Holism*.

The Identity Changing Dreams of a Schizoaffective Man
In an inpatient facility, the attending physician referred a Schizoaffective man to me. Throughout his life his disease had tormented him and tempted him to despair. For years, this sixty-two year old Irish Catholic man had suf-

fered both from the symptoms of manic depression as well as lapses into the
delusions and hallucinations that characterize paranoid schizophrenia. Despite the fact that his psychiatrist had sensibly medicated him on antipsy-
chotic medication, he feared relapsing again. His fear was not unrealistic. In
the last five years, he had suffered relapses of mood and psychotic symptoms
that left him frightened and in need of an overhauled regimen of antipsy-
chotic medication. Two years before we began our work, he had gradually
begun to reclaim his religious faith. Daily he read the catechism and weekly
he attended mass. He was also faithful in his prayers. In therapy, he confided
to me that, while he found the renewed practice of his faith comforting, he
still feared his mental illness and had difficulty conceptualizing where God
was in the midst of his affliction. Then he reported the following dream:

> On a dark night, I walk through dimly lit streets. A cat-like creature
> stalks me in the darkness. I feel it gaining ground. The creature closes
> in on me. I am very nervous. Then I see a fence. A little, narrow en-
> trance way is the only means through the fence. As I get closer, the
> night watchman undoes a security barrier to the entrance. I slip
> through the tiny gate. Then the night watchman closes up the entrance
> just before the cat-like creature catches up with me. Feeling safe from
> the creature, I relax and look about the protected, fenced-in compound.
> I realize that this facility is a power company's power plant.

We conducted the dream interpretation collaboratively, treating the dream
allegorically and following his associations to find their meaning. The cat-
like creature represented the devil, described by St. Peter as a "lion looking
for someone to devour" (1 Pet. 5:8). This man had been tempted to lose faith
and despair that God would protect him in the face of his recurrent mental
illness. The cat-like creature represented the devouring quality of the bedev-
iling despair. The narrow gate, however, represented his escape from loosing
hope. Since this man had resumed his Christian practice, he had entered
through the narrow way into the kingdom of God. Since Jesus watches over
his flock, we recognized Christ as the night watchman, welcoming this man
into the protection of the kingdom of God. Because the dream concluded in a
power plant, the man realized that he was under the protection of God's
kingdom, a kingdom that generates tremendous protective power on his behalf. For him, the most important point of the dream concerned the revelation that God protected him from despair in the midst of his recurrent illness,
despite the fact that his illness remained a thorn in his flesh.

Six weeks after this dream, our interpretation was put to the test. The
man's symptoms returned, and he was hospitalized in a psychiatric ward for
some time. I felt concerned about him, but upon his return from the hospital,
he in fact did not succumb to the faith-destructive belief that Our Lord had

abandoned him. The Holy Spirit had arranged his dream and its meaning for him. The deep meaning inherent in his dream's symbols, offered him understanding, allegorically designed for him by the Holy Spirit, to ward off despair that would make him interpret his recurrent mental illness as God's abandonment. "To the contrary," he told me as we resumed our sessions, "God has been protecting me in the midst of this disease." As a practitioner of *Christian Holism*, I would have been satisfied at this statement. After all, my patient experienced the Holy Spirit's management of therapy so that he received an astonishing dream that warded off a spiritually lethal collapse of faith. But God's pursuit of this man's rejuvenation persisted. Just days after his discharge from the psychotic unit, he dreamt again.

> *I am aware of a Presence. I look and see Jesus. At first, I am afraid. Then I feel his love for me. It is enormous and strong. Jesus' love for me affirms me so completely that I love him back deeply. Jesus leaves me, but the experience of his love is indelible. Something in me has changed.*

This dream did change him. While the first dream promised protection from despair, this dream left him with an unshakable understanding of his importance to Our Lord. Even weeks following this dream, the man felt deeply moved by his new identity—a beloved man of Christ. Together, these two dreams shifted him from the temptation to interpret his psychiatric situation as God's abandonment, to the realization, not only of God's protection and acceptance, but most importantly of his beloved status, his specialness to Jesus. A third dream in this series came shortly.

> *I enter a boxing ring. I wear boxing gear and am ready to fight. I hear my father yell, "Fight for Ireland and the faith." When I wake up, I feel determined.*

This final dream was important. Exploring the symbols, we agreed that his father's voice represented God the Father's encouragement for the man to spiritually fight for the liberation of human spiritual ground occupied by forces of darkness. By continuing in his acts of devotion, this man participates in the fight that ultimately liberates God's creation from the forces of darkness—a fight that will also liberate him from his own illness, either in this life or the next. A beautiful point is that the dream dignifies the man with the status of a spiritual fighter. The dream provides him with an identity of a Christian soldier, rather than as a mentally ill man. This dream-given identity as an earthly fighter for the kingdom of God, preserved him (and me) from the temptation to lose his real identity to his illness. The dream prevented us from falsely basing his identity on his Schizoaffective disorder,

God used this dream in such a way that this young therapist gained powerful insight into his woundedness and his need for God's Holy Spirit to refresh his dry soul.

as many survivors of mental disorders do. At this writing, he practices Christianity with dignity and aggressive faithfulness. He rightly believes that, despite the mystery of his suffering, he is under God's protection, deeply loved by Jesus, and has been commissioned to fight the good fight through his devotions. Importantly, he identifies himself as a Christian soldier, rather than as a Schizoaffective.

The Unmasking Dream of the Therapist Thirsty for Love

A twenty-eight year old graduate student came to me for treatment. A disturbing dream upset his enjoyment of his postdoctoral work at a prestigious university. Prior to the dream, this bright Presbyterian man had enjoyed the mentorship of some of the most important psychologists in the world. He had access to them on a daily basis, discussed his cases with them, and enjoyed their confidence. He thought of himself as a future luminary in his profession. At times, he found himself feeling sorry for his patients who could not always understand his brilliant psychological analyses. At other times, he found himself inpatient with clients' failure to progress at the pace he had set for them. Despite such frustrations, he found his budding professional success satisfying, especially because he had came from an unpromising background that included poverty and humiliation in grade school due to an undiagnosed learning disability. The following dream, however, changed his relationship to himself and to his work:

I eat dinner at home. Two priests interrupt my meal. They tell me that a dying man needs my help. They take me to a room. I see two generals guarding a dying man. The generals wear tunics covered with medals. They look grand and self-satisfied. Then, I examine the dying man. He lies naked on a mat. Dehydration has so overtaken his body that parts of him have mummified. He looks at me and exudes misery. Then he hands me a newspaper advertisement. The advertisement reads, "Send away for an occult incantation. This incantation will help you to become a Superman. Then everyone will love you." I realize that this poor guy has bought into this occult message. Hoping to become a Superman, he sent for the occult incantation only to find that the incantation brought a curse upon him instead of the love he sought. Superman was an idol, a false god. I realize that if decisive action is not taken for this poor guy on the mat, he will quickly die from lack of love. I start yelling at the priests and the generals to pray for the poor guy. The generals look like they can't be bothered. They want to look good and disdain the distasteful task of praying for the dehydrated guy. The priests look more concerned, but they really don't know how to pray for this poor, loveless guy. They're clueless. Concerned for the abject misery of the naked dying man, I wake up horrified.

Emotional alarm and pain initially emerged in the wake of the dream. This man had a nightmare. His soul was in a state of emergency. His disturbing dream alerted him to the need for decisive healing action. Following prayer, we addressed the dream allegorically and used his associations to understand it. The priests interrupted his meal, his regular routine, to show him that a part of himself was dying. As he got close to the dying part of himself, he saw the generals. They symbolized his identification with the power and prestige associated with his privileged academic status. He used his prestigious position to erect a false identity—an identity of an invulnerable person. The generals represented his defensive, false identity that guarded the real problem. In the dehydrated man, he recognized the hurt part from which he sought to escape. But the dream prevented him from hiding in the false identity of an impressive person. He saw within himself a part mortally thirsting for love and approval and deeply hurt from the school-age humiliation brought on by his learning disability. That this figure of lovelessness and humiliation embodied itself as dehydrated shows the need these wounds had of the healing, loving, refreshment of the Holy Spirit that Jesus described as "living water" (Jn 7:38). Unwittingly, he had succumbed to the occult notion that he could save himself from his woundedness and fallenness by achieving tremendous worldly accomplishment. In the midst of this accomplishment, God gave him this dream to show him that his ideal self was nothing more than an idolatrous pursuit. Even if he did become superman, superman would not bring love and healing to his soul. Superman would not earn enough medals or become so grand as to transcend the deeply human need for the living water of God's restorative grace. This man realized that he needed God's love to heal, not a lot of pompous, worthless worldly success. In the dream, the generals were impervious to this realization, and the priests did not know what to do about it. This showed that his false self was entrenched in his soul and that his Christian faith needed maturation before healing could occur.

My client and I identified this dream as a Big Dream, because it mapped the course of healing for some time to come. Quickly, however, the impact of the dream led to several therapeutic changes. First, he owned that he overvalued a self-image of professional success and brilliance as a way to gain acceptance and love from himself and others. When he acknowledged that this project failed and had almost killed him spiritually, he found that his relationship to his patients had changed. He no longer experienced disdain or impatience when patients did not understand or appreciate his "brilliance." And when eventually, he gave up trying to be a brilliant therapist altogether, he was surprised that God had blessed him with the gift of compassion. Ultimately, his clients were just plain getting better, and he was less concerned with being "brilliant." By being less the General and more the humble man in need of living water, he had become a better therapist and a more-healed person.

When he left treatment, he had developed much more genuine humility and presented himself as personally more real. Aware of his need to strengthen his faith, he began to pray and read the Bible more regularly. He also made it a point to develop fellowship with people who would support his project. Most importantly, he turned from seeking false ways to restore his soul and sought healing by repeatedly inviting the living water of the Holy Sprit to stream into those dehydrated soul-places in which he thirsted for healing love. He was healing and so were his patients. God used this dream in such a way that this young therapist gained powerful insight into his woundedness and his need for God's Holy Spirit to refresh his parched core. Others in this young man's healing care were direct beneficiaries of his abandonment of personal falseness. The dream helped him and others.

The Dream of the Woman Who Needed to Get Free from Her Dependency and Get On With Her Life

A colleague of mine asked me to consult with her on a case. She referred me to a distressed 55 year old woman. This client suffered from debilitating dependency issues that stemmed from her childhood. She had never known her father, and her mother, a distressed person in her own right, was unable to care for her. Her mother would go to "parties" for days at a time, leaving her very young daughter to fend for herself. Due to her unmet dependency needs, this woman grew up feeling that she lacked the strength to mange her life without someone to take care of her. In her mid twenties, she married, and the anxious dread that interminably plagued her subsided. For several years, she enjoyed a relatively normal life. She loved her husband, and they had a baby girl. By her early thirties, however, the marriage deteriorated and her husband left, leaving her emotionally devastated with a child to raise alone. As her own daughter matured, this woman clung to her more and more, depending on her daughter for constant reassurance and a social life. Temperamentally independent, the daughter increasingly recoiled from her mother's neediness. Finally, in an argument filled with recrimination, the daughter broke with her mother, accusing her of making unreasonable demands and reversing appropriate mother/daughter roles. Hurt by her daughter's rejection, she entered treatment with my colleague. In the course of therapy, she had difficulty owning that she relied inappropriately on her daughter, and she despaired of living a happy life without her daughter to closely rely upon. Therapy reached a standstill, and her depression became alarmingly acute. This woman's therapist, my colleague, an immensely talented psychologist trained in both secular and sacred therapy, then asked me to assess her client and to make treatment recommendations. (Relying on one another this way is customary in our practice.)

My colleague briefed me, and then I consulted with her client. We prayed, and the woman discussed her sense of discouragement with her life, and her wish that the therapeutic work in which she and my colleague were engaged would go faster. From a technical point of view their therapy was fine. They were engaged in "working through" early abandonment, reworking thoughts related to dependency issues, and modifying behavior that involved developing social supports apart from her daughter. Yet, her depression persisted. She had a sense that her therapy would not work if her daughter did not support her. She also had a sense that without her daughter's help it was inevitable that she would be unhappy. This idea preoccupied her and was not susceptible to cognitive restructuring. In the midst of this discussion, she remarked that she had a dream and wondered if it was important to the topic.

I stand on a cliff above a river. With me on the cliff are seals. The seals are in single file. The first seal stands at the very edge of the cliff, the next one just behind, and so on. The line of seals stretches from the cliff to the horizon. Then the first seal jumps off the cliff and lethally smashes on the rocks below. Then the next seal does the same. The seals keep jumping off the cliff and dying on the rocks. They do this over and over. Next, I fall off the cliff. But I do not land on the rocks like the seals. I land in the river. The current is strong, and I think that I will be swept away. I see my daughter. For a moment I feel relieved. I know if I swim to her I will be safe. But she swims away from me. Then I feel sad and fearful. I think that I will drown. The current takes me down stream. I realize that I can float and ride the current.

Together, we interpreted her dream, associating to the symbols in the confidence that God would lead us to the meaning. The seals symbolized two meanings. First, they represented persistent suicide fantasies. In the face of her despair over reconciling with her daughter, the dying animals voiced the part of her that wished to kill the pain of her unmet dependency needs and her sense of abandonment. But the seals also had a life-giving meaning. This woman felt that with her daughter's rejection her fate had been "sealed." She felt that without her daughter's support, she could not live a happy life. Yet, the fact that the seals kept dying suggested that her fate was actually "unsealed." The "unsealing" seals repeated over and over the notion that she could thrive without her daughter's support. The image insisted, "Your fate is unsealed. Your fate is unsealed." The woman could live on her own. The next part of the dream put this idea to the test. She fell in the water, not on the rocks—another indicator that living without her daughter would not be as hard a let-down as she expected. Once in the river, though, she turned toward her daughter to keep her head above water. The daughter swam away—a dream sign reflecting what the woman already knew; she could not rely on her daughter to keep her from drowning in her fear of abandonment. The woman would have to depend on herself—and, in fact, she could. She did not drown. She rode the current. She had the capacity to go with the flow of her life without depending on her daughter as her life preserver.

This dream was important. In symbolic language, it showed to my colleague and her client that their therapy had been on track, that in fact the insights and interventions they had developed were in the right direction, taking the client from a death position to a life position. As it was, the dream gave advance notice regarding the direction that the woman's life would take in response to treatment. In the weeks following the dream, my colleague and her client, continued to work, and the woman's depression lessened. She began to focus less on her daughter. She began to develop interests of her own. And she found the ego strength to keep her head above water and to go with the flow without having to rely as much on others. As a practitioner of *Christian Holism*, I find it significant that this woman's dream was dreamt in the context of prayer, interpreted in the context of prayer, and provided a lasting, healing metaphor to encourage and guide her treatment. These visible signs of grace suggested to me that the Holy Spirit was therapeutically present in my colleague's treatment, the woman's dream, the interpretative dream work and its aftermath.

The Exoneration/Healing Dream of the Bereaved Mother

A brilliant, thirty-eight-year-old professional Methodist woman entered treatment for anxiety. Talented, accomplished, and very smart, she presented as polished and poised; yet, a maddening sense of dread plagued her subjectivity. For months, she suffered from a feeling that something was terribly wrong. Her body was tense, and she had difficulty concentrating. She was easily startled, and, at night, insomnia tormented her. She searched her mind for what might be wrong, but she found nothing. In frustration, she sought psychotherapy. Initially, finding no source for her anxiety, we discussed the possibility that her problem might stem from a physical cause, requiring psychiatric, rather than psychological treatment. Prayer and persistence, however, amount to powerful therapeutic virtues, and, finally, our therapy bore fruit. (The Holy Spirit always blesses faithful work.)

"You know," said the woman. "I am not married. And over the years, I had several important, long-term romantic relationships with men I expected to marry. In three of these relationships, I fell so in love and felt so secure in the relationship that I allowed myself to become pregnant, expecting that we would marry and raise the child together. Each time, however, my pregnancy so overwhelmed the fathers, that they abandoned me. Feeling unable to raise children on my own and fearing social disgrace, I aborted each of the three pregnancies."

Having a strong background in medicine, it was easy for this woman to rationalize that each fetus amounted to no more than a mass of tissue, not a real person. Yet, a part of her yearned to love her terminated pregnancies as children. She felt guilt and horror at the course she had taken during those earlier, desperate times. From a clinical perspective, her anxiety emerged from the conflict of what she consciously believed—that the abortions were necessary and justifiable—and what she believed in an unconscious, deeply maternal chamber of her soul—that she unnecessarily lost the opportunity to love her valuable children. When the Holy Spirit brought this insight to us, the woman's pain became acute. She wept inconsolably as she took owner-ship of the guilt she felt for the abortions and for the grief she felt as she ter-ribly missed her lost little ones.

She reflected that she saw her abortions as a mistaken path for which she would like to ask forgiveness from God. Importantly, I do not have a highly developed relationship to the issue of abortion, so her desire to address the problem of her abortions through forgiveness-seeking emerged from the Spirit's work in the treatment process, rather than my own agenda. This made her prayer all the more meaningful. She asked God for forgiveness and experienced lessening of her guilt. Her grief, however, remained quite acute. She said that she still missed her children and wished that there was some-thing she could do for them. We discussed the matter and decided that she could minister to them by committing their souls to Jesus in prayer. These prayers were both funereal and baptismal. In this manner, we prayed and this brave woman left therapy exhausted.

Following this breakthrough session, I reflected that the Holy Spirit had worked a dramatic amount of progress in her therapy. The Holy Spirit un-covered the source of her anxiety disorder—repressed guilt and grief emer-gent from three terminated pregnancies. The Sprit also convicted her of the wrongness of the abortions and blessed her with forgiveness. And the Spirit blessed her with a way to minister to the children by committing her chil-dren's souls to Christ. Satisfied with her therapeutic progress, I was unpre-pared for the way God offered even greater healing.

In the next session, she told me that she left therapy and went home. Ex-hausted, she lay in bed, fell asleep, and slipped into a dream.

In the dream I look into heaven and see Jesus. He holds each of my children. With playfulness and love, he jostles them in his arms. My

While psychotherapy helped her to recover from anxiety emergent from her repressed guilt and grief, the dream represented the Holy Spirit's sovereign confirmation of her exoneration and healing—and blessed her to fulfill herself by loving her children.

three kids love it. It is so apparent that everyone is okay, and they are having a wonderful time—and that Jesus himself loves and enjoys these kids immensely. Then I realize that my children and Jesus look to me. No accusation comes from the kids, and no condemnation comes from Jesus. They beam at me and smile. In words of thought, Jesus tells me that the guilt and grief I have felt about the abortions has ended. Jesus tells me that he has heard my prayer. He will raise my children for me in heaven. I see that he is doing this. Best of all, Jesus invites me to love the kids again. I do love them, and I love loving them. And the children love me from heaven.

We discerned that the Spirit had given her the dream for two reasons: one, to offer her a glimpse into heaven that confirmed that God had answered her prayer to care for her children's souls; and two, to fully heal her guilt and grief by allowing her to love her children with maternal love. The dream was a therapeutic turning point. Her symptoms diminished, so treatment soon concluded. Later, she experienced occasional flare-ups of guilt and grief, but, by using the dream as an internal icon, she could recover from these symptoms and emerge to enjoy loving her kids. While psychotherapy helped her to recover from anxiety emergent from her repressed guilt and grief, the dream represented the Holy Spirit's sovereign confirmation of her exoneration and healing—and blessed her to fulfill herself by loving her children. Recently, I heard that she lives quite happily and helps women with similar issues.

The Attorney's Dream of Shattered Narcissism and Christ's Healing

A 42-year-old, Lutheran attorney called for an appointment. Married with 4 children, he had for years striven to establish his law firm as the preeminent practice in his area. His motto was: "Nothing succeeds like work-a-holism"- and his firm grew large. He hired bright associates and enjoyed immense success. In his privileged position, he felt self-congratulatory and attributed his success to his shrewdness and brilliance. He enjoyed making money. He enjoyed being professionally on top. And he enjoyed (secretly) looking down on people of "poor judgment and low mentality" who hired him to defend their interests in the face of their ridiculous, pathetic mistakes. As Christmas approached, he threw an expensive, firm-wide party to celebrate a year of record breaking revenues. Dressed to the hilt, he showed up with his beautiful wife on his arm. But early in the evening, his introverted wife became tired and left. The attorney waved her off, made merry, and drank heavily. The drunker he got, the more convinced he became that a female associate was attracted to him. In a moment of clarity, he thought to check himself but drank another whiskey. Under the pretext of discussing a case, the attorney isolated her in a room adjacent to the ballroom and threw a clumsy pass at her. This repulsed and offended his associate. She dislodged his pawing hands and slapped her boss across the face. She wheeled away, remarking, "This is harassment, and I have a case." The attorney was devastated.

In the days that followed, the lawyer feared a scandal or a lawsuit that would jeopardize his professional standing. He further agonized at the disconnect between his exploitive, intoxicated lechery and his preferred self-image of a meritorious man whose urbanity allowed him to stand above the mistakes of others. Unable to metabolize his fear or to regulate his self esteem, he longed to confide in his wife, but he had betrayed her, so he remained silent. Finally, fearing that his distractedness would compromise his functioning, he sought consultation.

In therapy, we established rapport and defined the problem as crippling shame and guilt over his behavior. The fact that he had "behaved stupidly" wounded his self image, and he remained fearful of reprisal from his offended associate—and, hence, he suffered from anxiety. He also remarked—somewhat humorously—that he was "neither a good Christian, nor a successful sinner." This important remark triggered an association to the following dream he had dreamt the previous, fitful night.

> *I stand on the top of a mountain. I see in every direction. I feel exultant. Something goes wrong, and I fall into a slide of rough cement. Gravity pulls me. I slide down the mountain fast. As I try to slow myself, friction burns and bleeds my hands. Down the mountain, I plummet. At bottom, I fly from the slide and land hard on rocks. My spine snaps, and I am paralyzed. Pipes pour sewage around my immobile body. I'm splattered with offal. On near rocks, at eye level, a crowd gathers. People I judge as losers and fools comprise the crowd. A man stands among the derelicts and helps them. The guy is Sting, the rock star. I try to move but cannot. Sting fixes his gaze into my eyes and commands "Get up and walk." I am released from my paralysis and healed. I get up and run away, afraid of Sting.*

Reflecting on the dream, the attorney realized that it symbolically condensed his current problem. Until recently, he thought of himself as above other people, on top of the heap. His professional success supported this narcissistic self exultation—the experience of being a high-up person high on himself. But neither his accomplishments nor his narcissism could protect him from the gravitational pull of his fallen nature. Drunk at his own party, he had gone ethically, morally, and professionally down hill. He could not check himself against the momentum of his intoxication and lust. The realization that he had jeopardized his professional standing, harassed an associate, betrayed his wife, and trespassed against his religious values, paralyzed him with shame, guilt, and fear. So damaging had been his mistake that he was incapable of healing or moving from his brokenness without assistance. Adding insult to narcissistic injury was the fact that he could no longer view himself as above others. Covered in filth at the bottom of the mountain, he was as dirty and low as the people he had judged unworthy. He was a person at the bottom of the heap among the refuse of human mistakes.

A practicing Christian, the attorney understood that forgiveness and healing (and guidance as to how to make restitution to his associate and wife) resided in Christ. And the Sting figure obviously represented the true Christ. But why of all the potential Christ figures, Sting? In high school, enthused by Police albums, the attorney recalled, he used to irreverently quip, "Sting is God." Recollecting this, the attorney felt sheepish and humbled and grateful that God had a sense of humor. For the attorney, the dream ultimately reiterated the ongoing Christian realization that we are not self-sufficient pseudo-gods, that we all sin, and that Jesus Christ forgives our sins and heals us of the paralyzing brokenness which we sustain from our ruinous behavior.

With moving self-honesty, the attorney interpreted his *flight* behavior at the dream's conclusion in the following manner:

> I'm desperate enough to accept Christ's healing, but I'm too allergic to my own shame to stay and talk with the guy who heals me. Even though spending time with Jesus would be good for me, the fear of what I might learn about myself or what Jesus might ask of me makes me run away. What if Jesus asked me to seek forgiveness from my associate or my wife? I couldn't handle it.

The attorney understood the dream as a metaphor for his true condition. He was called to abandon his pride, admit he had fallen, view himself as another sinner, and acknowledge that forgiveness and healing come from Jesus Christ. He reaffirmed his Christian commitment and vowed to be a humbler boss and a better husband. When his anxiety diminished, he left treatment. The issues of his obligation to his associate and wife, along with his fear of closeness to God, were left under-addressed. Whenever I hear Sting on the radio, however, I am reminded that God knows this man better than anyone, and that the Great Therapist knows exactly how to bless him.

Conclusion

Christian Holism values dream work. In scripture, dreams have been instrumental in blessing God's people. Important Church fathers thought highly of dreams and believed that God used dreams for good purposes. Both Pope Leo IX and Constantine dreamt important dreams in which they received divine communication. In *Christian Holism*, knowledge of scripture and tradition as well as social science informs the practitioner's understanding of dreams. Yet, the practitioner appreciates that it is the clinical presence of the Holy Spirit that blesses this knowledge, works with it, and even supersedes it. In *Christian Holism*, the Spirit works within the dream work between the therapist and the client to unlock the grace contained within the vision—all for the purpose of healing.

Reference Notes

1. Important neurologists have begun to re-appreciate the supposition regarding the therapeutic value of dreams. Solms (2004) writes, "psychological conceptualizations of dreaming have become scientifically respectable again" (p. 88). Hobson (2004) asserts, "We have always argued that dreams are emotionally salient and meaningful" (p.89).
2. In my own practice of *Christian Holism*, I find that cognitive-behavioral methods of dreamwork are excellent from the point of view of technique. The questions I ask are: "If the actions and actors of the dream are ideas that the client holds about herself in the world, what exactly are those ideas? And, once found, how can those ideas be leveraged or restructured to help the client reach her treatment goals?" An additional resource is the Spring, 2002 issue of The Journal of Cognitive Therapy, which is a special issue that deals with Cognitive Therapy and dreams

References

Brewer, E.C. (1992). *A dictionary of miracles*. Philadelphia, PA: J.B. Lippincott Co.

Hobson, A. (2004). Freud Returns Like a Bad Dream. *Scientific American, 5*, 290, 89

Lewis, J. (1995). *The dream encyclopedia.* Washington, D.C.: Visible Ink.

Savary, L., Berne, P., and Williams, S.K. (1984). *Dreams and spiritual growth: A Judeo-Christian way of dreamwork.* New York: Paulist Press.

Solms, M. (2004). Freud Returns. *Scientific American, 5*, 290, 82-88.

Psycho-Energetic Psychotherapy*

Charles L. Zeiders, Psy.D.

Growing interest in psycho-energetic therapies makes it important for the Christian therapist to understand that Christian psychotherapy has psycho-energetic dimensions, that is, components of therapy that concern energy and recognize it as part of
the healing enterprise. This article traces Christian psycho-
energetic healing form its origins in the first century, to the development of a healing tradition, and eventually to some of the
documented and unmistakably psycho-energetic healing experiences of the twentieth century. Care has been taken to frame
this look at Christian healing through the eyes of credible, practical theologians, among them Agnes Sanford and Francis
MacNutt.

C hristian counselors and therapists have become aware of a rise in
interest in psycho-energetic therapy. Psycho-energetic therapy consciously deals with a subtle healing force or energy in the pursuit of healing
for the client. Bio-energetics, Core energetics, Therapeutic Touch, Acupuncture, and Yoga are all examples of such therapies.[1] In light of this, it is important for Christian therapists to realize that a tremendous legacy of psycho-
energetic healing inheres in the Christian tradition. As the following article
makes clear, God has vast resources that can enter into the healing enterprise, sometimes as a palpable, perceptible flowing force, as therapists imitate Jesus Christ by participating in His healing ministry.

Oskar Estebany, who "felt that he was a channel for Jesus the
Christ" (Krieger, 1979, p.6), had a reputation as a healer of people, and has
participated in several well documented, tightly controlled studies with mice.
Experimental mice suffering from wounds and malnutrition responded to
Estebany's healing technique in such a way that experimental results were
statistically significant and in the direction of health (Murphy, 1992). The
Roman Catholic Estebany believed that an *energy* passed from him to his
patients (Rorvik, 1974).

Like Estebany, a number of Christian therapists believe that certain spiritual interventions can decisively impact the mental and physical health of
their clients. These interventions are prayer and the laying on of hands. Inherited from the Christian religious tradition, these healing practices are utilized by theologically minded psychologists and counselors to move some

---

* This article was first published in *The Journal of Christian Healing*, Volume 18, #3, Fall, 1996, pp. 3-15.

force, usually configured as the grace or power of God, into the client's psychological wound. Once a Christian healer introduces God's grace to the wounded psychological area, it begins to re-order in such a way that it conforms to God's image of mental health for that person. In this article, I will trace the development of Christian healing and discuss its theory and practice with an emphasis on its energetic component. Naturally, any such discussion begins with Jesus.

Jesus of Nazareth: Healer

Holy Writ guides Christian thinking about psycho-energetic healing. From scriptural records, Christians learn that part of imitating Jesus Christ is to heal people. This is because so much of the New Testament involves Jesus intervening to restore dysfunctional minds and bodies. For instance, in Mark's Gospel, which most scholars believe was the primary source for Matthew and Luke, 209 verses out of 666 are about the healing miracles of Jesus. That is just over 31 percent (Grazier, 1989, p. 82).

Similarly, assuming that the ancient writings are correct, one sees in Jesus a man with a very definite healing mission. According to the four Gospels Jesus healed:

- Four cases of blindness: Bartimaeus (Mark 10:46; Matthew 20:29-34; Luke 18:35-43); the blind man of Bethsaida (Mark 8:22-26); two blind men (Matthew 9:27-31); and the man blind from birth (John 9:1-34).
- Two cases of fever: Peter's mother-in-law (Matthew 8:14-15; Mark 1:30-31; Luke 4:38-39); and the official's son (John 4:46-54).
- Eleven lepers: a single leper (Matthew 8:1-4; Mark 1:40-45; Luke 5:12-16) and ten lepers (Luke 17:11-19).
- A deaf mute (Mark 7:31-37).
- A woman with a hemorrhage (Matthew 9:20-22; Mark 5:25-34; Luke 8:43- 48).
- A man with a withered hand (Matthew 12:9-13; Mark 3:1-5; Luke 6:6-10).
- A man with dropsy (Luke 14:1-6).
- A centurion's servant with paralysis (Matthew 8:5-13; Luke 7:1-10).
- A wounded stave of the high priest (Luke 22:50-51).
- The sick of Capernaum (Matthew 8:16-17; Mark 1:32-34, Luke 4:40-41).
- Many people from Tyre, Sidon, and Galilee (Matthew 12:15-21; Mark 3:7-12; Luke 6:17-19).
- Those by the shore at Gennesaret (Matthew 14:34-36; Mark 6:53-54).
- The sick at Bethsaida (Matthew 14:14; Luke 9:1-11) and at Tiberius (John 6:2).
- Crowds at entering Judea (Matthew 19:2), (Murphy, 1992, pp. 260-261)

Once a Christian healer introduces God's grace to the wounded psychological area, it begins to reorder in such a way that it conforms to God's image of mental health for that person.

For the Christian therapist, to be like Jesus is to be a healer, and imitating the healing ministry of the Nazarene has psycho-energetic implications. Christ's healings imply that he had the power to conduct some kind of positive energy into his subject's wounds. This idea is illustrated in the story of the healing of the woman with a hemorrhage.

A large crowd followed and pressed around him. And a woman was there who was subject to bleeding for twelve years. She had suffered a great deal under the care of many doctors and had spent all she had, yet instead of getting better she grew worse. When she heard about Jesus, she came up behind him in the crowd and touched his cloak, because she thought, "If I just touch his clothes, I will be healed." Immediately her bleeding stopped and she felt in her body that she was freed from her suffering. At once Jesus realized that *power* had gone out from him. (*The New International Version Study Bible*, 1985, Mark: 5:24-31; p. 1503; italics mine).

Some scholars propose that in the above event Jesus felt an energetic force move as a healing vitality from his body to the body of the hemorrhaging woman. In the original Greek, the word translated as "power" is *dynamis* "which has to be understood as the power of the Lord to heal" (Fitzmyer, 1981, p 744). The Anglican priest Harpur (1994), however, suggests a different translation of *dynamis*; instead of translating the word as *power*, Harpur would have the word translated as *energy*. Harpur's discussion of Jesus' healing ministry portrays Jesus as a conduit for a healing energy that proceeds from the mind of the God whose concern is for the wellness of His children.

... in healing the sick [Jesus was] an agent or channel for the Divine Energy flowing from the heart of the universe, the very breath or presence of the dynamic Spirit of God. (p.60-61)

Jesus healed, at least in part, via a divine energy, and his followers began to do the same.

The Development of Healing After Jesus

James, the brother of Jesus and head of the Jerusalem church, also believed that God made healing power available to believers through the avenues of touch and prayer. Harpur's interpretation of James' instructions re-

garding healing techniques is especially enlightening, because it lays bare
the interaction of mind, body, energy, and health.

> In the fifth chapter [of his epistle] James writes, "Is any among you ill?
> Let him call for the church elders and let them pray over him, anointing
> him with oil in the name of the Lord. And the prayer of faith will save
> the sick and the Lord will raise him up. And if he has committed sins
> they will be forgiven him. Admit your faults to one another and pray
> for each other that you may be healed. The active prayer of a just per-
> son has an enormous effect" (James 5:13-16).
>
> In addition to underlining the fact that healing, through prayer and
> anointing with oil, was considered normal in the primitive Christian
> Church, this passage gives further witness to the near universal reli-
> gious conviction that there can be times when an illness may be the
> result ... of unresolved sins or faults. An obvious example would be
> problems created by deliberate abuse of one's body through neglect ...
> But James is not implying that sickness and disease are always some-
> how a sign of wrong-doing ... What James is stressing is that confes-
> sion of known sins—a frank facing up to the specific times and places
> when one has fallen short of what one knows one should have done or
> been—and the assurance of forgiveness remove the spiritual blockages
> that prevent healing energy from flowing in (pp. 70-71).

What Harpur clarifies here is the apostle's contention that psychological
conditions influence an individual's ability to receive energy and heal.

The *Acts of the Apostles,* written by the physician Luke who had a keen
interest in healing, records healings accomplished through St. Peter and St.
Paul. These healing events appear to have implicit psycho-energetic components. In these stories, touch, prayerful intention, and the unleashing of healing power converge. Writing to the fledgling church at Corinth, St. Paul em-
phasized that the Holy Spirit gives healing power to believers and the ability
to perform "deeds of power." According to biblical accounts, there were
times when articles of clothing which the apostles touched conveyed healing
power to sick people. From a scientific point of view, these stories are not
unlikely.

> Evidence from studies of healing with plants and animals indicates
> that healing may be conveyed by such vehicles as water and cotton
> wool. This is consonant with ... reports dating back to the Bible, when
> Christ and the Apostles gave healing through handkerchiefs. Modern
> day healers confirm ... that this works well (Benor, 1992, P. 74).

The apostles may have been able to endow articles of clothing with healing energy, which in turn could be conveyed to the sick through the application of the energized garment to the person to be healed. Regardless of the mechanisms involved, however, healing became a vital part of the early Church and became a permanent part of the Christian tradition.

The Development of the Tradition

In the centuries following the Ascension, church fathers and many saints solidified the position that the healing *dynamis* flows through healers and cures physical and psychological pathologies. They viewed a person's ability to heal others as a present from God, often bestowed to the believer at the time of baptism (McDonnell and Montague, 1991). The great spiritual geniuses of the early Church wrote enthusiastically about such power,

> Justin Martyr wrote in AD 165, "In our city, many Christian friends have been healed and have healed other sick persons in Jesus' name."
> Bishop Ireneus wrote in AD 180, "...those who truly are His disciples receive grace from Him to perform miracles in His name and they really cast out evil spirits. Others pray for the sick by laying hands on them and see them healed."
> Origin wrote in AD 250, "Some prove through healings that they perform what tremendous power they have through faith, in that they do not call on any other name over those who need help than the name of Jesus and God. In this manner we have seen many persons delivered from terrible misfortunes and mental disorders and innumerable other sicknesses...."
> In AD 275, Clement gave the following advice to young preachers, "Let them, therefore, with prayer and fasting pray for people in faith and trust in God ... as men who have received gifts to heal for God's glory" (Grazier, 1989, P. 77).

In the third century Hippolytus of Rome wrote that healers have a special status because they derive their gift from the Holy Spirit (Powers, 1985). Following Augustine's death in AD 430, the saint's friend and biographer Possidius wrote that Augustine recanted an earlier writing that healing had ceased, when he laid hands on a sick man whom God healed immediately following Augustine's touch (Gardner, 1986, P. 137).

Healers in History [2]

Healing became part of the Church's tradition and healers emerged from Church history. St. Patrick healed the blind. St. Bernard made the lame walk, the dumb speak, and the deaf hear. Edward the Confessor, King of England from 1042-66, healed scrofula by touching his afflicted subjects. In the mid 1600's Valentine Greatrakes gained notoriety in England for his ability to cure the sick. "[He] found to his amazement that he could cure epilepsy, pains ... and fevers, so that the people went home rejoicing and praising God" (Major, 1940, p. 169). Explaining his power Greatrakes remarked, "God gave my hand this gift" (p. 169). In historical records of Christian healings the experience of energy is often implied but frequently under-reported.

Christian Healing and the Experience of Energy
in the Twentieth Century

In this century the church (Christian therapists included among its members) continues to experience healings, but those exposed to gifts of healing tend to address the issue of energetic experience more directly than in the past. It should be noted, however, that even today very little literature directly addresses the experience of energy in the context of Christian psychotherapy. Reports of energy remain anecdotal, and when energy is addressed, it is rarely the main focus of articles or books.

The renowned healer Kathryn Kuhlman clearly had a gift. Medical case studies compiled by Casdorph (1976), show that some of those medically verified as healed by Kuhlman experienced energetic sensations described as "electrical" during her services. For example, a bank executive diagnosed with kidney and bone cancer experienced "a sensation like electricity running throughout his body during the service" (p.99). Examining him, befuddled physicians noted "healing" of his cancer. Similarly, a seventy-eight year-old Ph.D. speech therapist with a well documented history of rheumatoid and osteoarthritis attended a Kuhlman service. She "had the feeling of an electric current going down the outside and the inside of my leg to the knee ... I was virtually in a trance. It was the most peaceful, joyful experience" (p, 109). Feeling healed, she discarded her leg braces and soon received a clean bill of health from her doctor.

Gardner (1986), like Casdorph, a physician, also compiled case studies of healings that he felt were medically reliable and miraculous. In some of these cases, there are reports of extraordinary healings characterized by an interrelationship of faith, healing touch, and the sensation of energy. One dramatic healing is that of a school teacher who lost his eyesight as the result of injurious exposure to intense photographic lights. Eye doctors despaired that the man would regain his sight, so, in desperation, he made an appointment with a Christian healer. He writes

When I went into the house I was filled with peace. I became relaxed in the presence of this total stranger and felt that I was no longer in despair, the situation was no longer hopeless. We spoke together, I told him of the accident, he told me of the healings that our Lord had channeled through him and we prayed together. There was no doubt in my

Regardless of the mechanisms involved, however, healing became a vital part of the early Church and became a permanent part of the Christian tradition.

mind that Jesus was in control of the situation. He laid hands on my head and over my eyes, but nothing dramatic happened, so I arranged to [meet with him again] (p. 33).

The teacher waited for five days, feeling confident that God would heal him. When he and the healer met again, something dramatic happened as soon as they prayed.

... as soon as his hands were placed on my head I experienced a sensation of power in the form of a greatly flowing electric current which flowed through his hands and through my skull. I also became aware of the most vivid and beautiful color blue ... even though my eyes were closed—and the color and the electric sensation persisted until his hands were removed ... I also experienced the most amazing feeling of strength and warmth passing, in a tingling sensation, through my fingers and into my wrists and arms ... I felt that I had been reborn into God's service and able to administer His healing power too (p. 33-34).

Healing, faith, and the sensation of energy converge in this unusual report. Given the dramatic fact that the flow of the *dynamis*, the power, the energy of healing was so strong in this report and in the reports regarding Kuhlman's healings, one cannot help wondering from a scientific perspective what measurable phenomena may have accompanied these theological experiences. Gerber (1988) notes that the hands of some healers, measured by SQUID technology, show electromagnetic field strength measured at one hundred times higher than normal body activity during healer associated conditions. A currently unanswered question is: Is increased electromagnetic activity a common component of the Christian healing experience? A review of the literature leaves one empty-handed.

The Two Seminal Influences
on Christian Psycho-Energetic Psychotherapy

Agnes Sanford and Francis MacNutt have had the most influence on Christian psychotherapists who pray for their clients' mental health and experience energy. Their books are widely read among such professionals, and MacNutt, still living, lectures on healing to ministers and therapists throughout the world.

Agnes Sanford (1972a), whose understanding of Christian healing became famous among Christian therapists, thought of divine healing as having a definite energetic component. She referred to the power that proceeds from the Holy Spirit as a "healing vibration" and a "divine current" (p.90). When laying hands on people and praying for them she experienced heat, electrical sensations, and vibrations (Riffel, personal communication, 1994). Addressing the relationship between divine energy and the importance of exercising healing gifts, Sanford wrote:

God's life is a flow—it is living water—it is active electricity—it is love vibrating at a definite wave length and intensity. In order to keep the current flowing we must give it as an outlet so that it can complete its circuit. If we do not do so, the channel of its flow becomes clogged and it runs more and more thinly and finally ceases altogether. (p.91)

To be a healer one must constantly be open to allowing the healing energy, a manifestation of God's love, flowing through one's being and into the world. Additionally, Sanford advanced an energetic viewpoint regarding the interactions of body, mind, and God.

The very chemicals contained in the body—"the dust of the earth"— live by the breath of God, by the primal energy, the original force that we call God. This being so, it is strange that we do not establish a closer connection with God in prayer, we would receive a more abundant flow of energy. The creative force that sustains us is increased within our bodies. (p. 18)

To Sanford healing others of physical infirmities and of mental problems was a natural outgrowth of prayerful communion with God.

Especially important about Sanford's contribution to psycho-energetic healing is the fact that she herself once suffered from debilitating depression. According to her autobiography (Sanford, 1972b), she struggled vainly against her dysphoria until an Episcopal priest placed his hands upon her head and prayed that she would psychologically heal. She did heal, and this inaugurated a ministry during which she had a special sensitivity to bringing holy, healing energy to the wounded mind in the name of Jesus Christ. She writes that when praying for others psychological problems, the healer should not tell the subject that faith is requisite to bringing God's healing energy into the afflicted portion of his mind.

If you will search the scriptures you will see that Jesus did not demand faith of one whose mind was darkened or disturbed. He did not require faith of Jairus' daughter or of the centurion's son or the maniac of

"God's life is a flow—it is living water—it is active electricity—it is love vibrating at a definite wave length and intensity." Agnes Sanford

Gadara. He took the power of God in His own hands and spoke for them the word of faith (Sanford, 1966, p. 41).

She also provided specific instructions for conducting healing energy into the disturbed mind. She insisted that the Christian healer of mental illness can pour into the disturbed person's mind

> ... the light and life of God through our own minds and bodies. For this purpose the laying on of hands in the sacramental way, upon the head, is most valuable ... I do not try to explain the actual radiation of life and light that comes through the human being, as light shines through the light bulb, for their minds [the minds of disturbed people] are too confused to understand. I do not explain that as my words reach their conscious minds, so God's words flow through my body and my hands into their bodies and reach the unconscious mind that is the storehouse of the emotions (pp. 43-44).

In Sanford's conception of psycho-energetic healing, neither faith nor insight based on verbal understanding is necessary for healing. The healer merely lays hands on the subject and allows the restorative *dynamis* to flow into the mind of the sufferer and to restore it.

MacNutt (1974), one of Sanford's disciples and Christendom's acknowledged living expert on psychological and physical healing, originally advised healers to expect occasional energetic sensations, including heat, trembling, and "something like an electric current" passing through them (p 304). In the years following that statement, MacNutt (1977) developed a more elaborate understanding of the nature of the energy.

> As Christians we know that we share the very life of God himself (in Catholic terminology: grace) and it makes sense that something of that life giving power in the physical order can be shared and communicated when we touch a sick person. It seems to me that this current of energy is what so many people feel when we pray for them ... The way I understand it ... is like this: the Christian shares the life of God himself ... The Father, Son, and the Holy Spirit live within us. Somehow (and here is my conjecture) the energy generated by this life can overflow, can be communicated and flow from one person to another through touching that other person. In all of us there are areas where

sickness, sluggishness and death are at work spiritually, emotionally, and physically. But when another Christian ... gathers around to pray, the life, the love and the healing power of Jesus can be transmitted to the sick person ... It's like God's radiation treatment. (pp. 3 7-3 9)

In MacNutt's view, God lives in the Christian. When a Christian prayerfully lays on hands, the love of the God who lives in him flows out in the form of healing energy.

Since developing these ideas and gaining confidence as a Christian healer, MacNutt has set up an institute for healing in Florida, staffed primarily by psychotherapists. The work of this institute is to encourage therapists and other helping professionals to develop a spiritual life that enables them to conduct the radiating power of Jesus into their clients and patients. MacNutt has cautioned that the experience of energy is not necessary for healing to occur, although it frequently accompanies the laying on of hands. MacNutt (1977) has also remarked that people in need of healing often require more than one session of prayer. They may need a course of treatment, just as cancer patients need a course of radiation treatment. This type of ongoing prayer he calls "soaking prayer" (p.39).

Who Practices Christian Psycho-Energetic Healing Today?

Christian psycho-energetic healing is practiced by pastoral counselors and by Christian psychotherapists. Interventions such as the laying on of hands continue. Pastoral counselors like the charismatic Father DiOrio (1984) of New York, recommend applying psychological principles to the problems of sick parishioners and, after establishing an empathic understanding of the client, praying for their psychological distress, usually laying on hands. DiOrio's experience is that an energy sensation can accompany the intervention.

Francis Schoeninger (1992) of the Institute for Christian Counseling and Therapy holds the position that energy, in her terminology *life energy*, moves from the Holy Trinity, through the therapist to the client. She asserts that a disruption of a person's internal, ordering energy can cause mental, physical, or spiritual distress.

In the dominion that God has given us and in the ordering of the line of authority, a way in which to begin to take authority over what is out of order [in the client] emerges. The line of authority through which *life energy* communicates our proper "being" is Godhead (Trinity), Holy Spirit (within the Trinity), to human spirit, then throughout our being (spirit, mind/emotion and physical body). Within each [aspect of human being] ... *life energy* flows connecting all to all, instructing and ordering. In an area that is restricted for any reason, and the message

"As Christians we know that we share the very life of God himself (in Catholic terminology: grace) and it makes sense that something of that life giving power in the physical order can be shared and communicated when we touch the sick person."
Francis MacNutt

[of the *life energy*] is not received correctly ... function ... and order can be disrupted (italics hers) (p. 15).

Schoeninger believes that God provides "blueprints" for a person's healthy mental, physical, and spiritual functioning. These blueprints are encoded in an energy that emanates from God and endows the human being. When, due to trauma, sin, disease, etc.., the ordering life energy is subverted, it needs to be reinvigorated by more divine energy. This divine energy comes from the Holy Spirit, through an intermediary like a therapist, and flows into the afflicted area wherein the original energetic blueprint has been degraded. Once re-energized, the client's mind or body begins to heal according to the divine plan encoded in the life energy. This may sound complicated but the intervention is simple. The therapist listens, understands the problem, then prays for the client (Schoeninger, personal communication, 1994).

Conclusion

Christian psycho-energetic healing began early in the Christian tradition. Healing prayers, at times accompanied by energy experiences, are recorded in the New Testament. Jesus Christ felt power or energy flow from him in the course of healing the hemorrhaging woman. The apostle James recommended a healing touch, combined with prayer to remove disease. St. Peter and St. Paul appeared to be capable of energizing garments with healing energy, a feat consistent with modern research findings. The church fathers believed that touch and prayer were honored by God in such a way that the healing energy was communicated to the sick. In modern times, energy experiences have accompanied medical miracles accomplished through healers like Katherine Kuhlman and others. Christian thinkers who have had the most impact on Christian therapists are Agnes Sanford and Francis MacNutt. Both were major influences on pastoral counseling. Both addressed, if briefly, the fact that energy appears to flow from God, through healers, into the sick, out of love, in the name of Jesus Christ. Today practitioners like Father DiOrio and Francis Schoeninger practice psycho-energetic healing from a Christian perspective and continue to advance its understanding.

Reference Notes

1. See Oschman (2000) for an excellent treatment of the scientific basis for such therapies. See p. [need to add page number] of this book for *Christian Holism*'s theologically orthodox, spiritually progressive approach to energy medicine.
2. Recent Scholarship (Palmer, 2001) shows that, beginning in 640 A.D., Nestorian Christian monks dialogued with the Buddhist and Taoist communities that flourished during the Tang Dynasty. Attempting to make their version of Christ's teachings intelligible to the Chinese mind, the Nestorian's wrote the Jesus Sutras, wherein the Nestorians depict a Jesus who strengthens his disciples by providing them with "qi" or invigorating life energy.

References

Barker, K. (Ed.). (1985). *The NIV study bible*. Grand Rapids, MI: Zondervan Bible Publishers.

Benor, D. (1992). Lessons from spiritual healing research and practice. *Subtle Energies*, 3, 1, 73-78.

Casdorph, H. (1976). *The miracles*. Plainfield, NJ: Logos International.

DiOrio, R. (1984). *Called to heal*. New York: Doubleday.

Fitzmyer, J. (1981). *The gospel according to Luke I-IV* (Vol. 28). New York: Doubleday.

Gardner, R. (1986). *Healing miracles: A doctor investigates*. London: Darton, Longman, and Todd.

Gerber, R. (1988). *Vibrational medicine*. Santa Fe: Bear & Company.

Grazier, J. (1989). *The power beyond*. New York: Macmillan.

Harpur, T. (1994). *The uncommon touch*. Toronto: McClelland & Stewart

Krieger, D. (1979). *The therapeutic touch: How to use your hands to help or heal*. Sante Fe, NM: Bear & Co.

Major, R. (1940). *Faiths that healed*. New York: Appleton-Century Company.

MacNutt, F. (1974). *Healing*. Notre Dame: Ave Maria Press.

MacNutt, F. (1977). *Power to heal*. Notre Dame: Ave Maria Press.

McDonnell, K. and Montague, G. (1991). *Christian initiation and baptism in the holy spirit*. Collegeville, MN: The Liturgical Press.

Murphy, M. (1992). *The future of the body*. New York: Putnam Publishing Group.

Oschman, J. (2000). *Energy medicine: The scientific basis*. Philadelphia, PA: Churchill Livingstone.

Palmer, M. (2001). *The Jesus sutras: Rediscovering the lost scrolls of Taoist Christianity*. New York: The Ballantine Publishing Group.

Powers, D. (1985). *Gifts that differ: Lay ministries established and unestablished*. New York: Pueblo Publishing Company.

Rorvik, D. (1974). The healing hand of Mr. E. *Esquire*, February, *70*, 154-60.

Sanford, A. (1972a). *The healing light*. New York: Ballentine Books.

Sanford, A. (1772b). *Sealed orders*. South Plainfield, NJ: Bridge Publishing.

Sanford, A. (1966). *The healing gifts of the spirit*. New York: Harper Collins.

Schoeninger, F. (1992). A Vision of Life Energy. *Journal of Christian Healing*, 14, 4, 12-16.

A Review of the Evidence Regarding the Behavioral Medical and Psychological Efficacy of Christian Prayer*

Charles L. Zeiders, M.S. and Ronald Pekala, Ph.D.

Prayer represents a vital component of modern life that influences psychological, bodily, and spiritual health. This article reviews psychological aspects of prayer and then explores the effects of prayer and prayer-like interventions upon biological systems. Next, evidence is explored which provides clues to the extent that prayer might influence the health of human and nonhuman organisms. Finally, the effects of prayer are discussed in light of a series of reviewed studies.

Introduction

Christian prayer, as a psychological and behavioral medical intervention, enjoys empirical, anecdotal, and theoretical support as a means to influence human behavior and experience. Yet, most mental health professionals are unaware of the effect that prayer exerts on biological and psychological systems. Hence, mental health professionals should familiarize themselves with the prayer literature, because the data shows that not only does prayer remain relevant to the world view of many clients and their communities, but prayer can exert a modest, but significant effect on biological and psychological systems.

Prayer remains an activity practiced by many Americans. According to Greeley (1991), survey data for the last half century shows that over 95 out of every 100 people profess belief in God, three out of four believe in life after death, three out of four accept the divinity of Jesus Christ, three out of five believe in hell, two out of five go to religious services (three out of five of those who are over forty), nine out of ten pray weekly, one out of two pray daily, and one out of four pray several times a day. The data depicts a spiritual populace, seeking God in prayer, looking for a special way to relate to the divine.

The fact that prayer plays a central role in Americans' dealing with psychological and medical issues finds expression in the popular media, cyber-

* This article was first published in *The Journal of Christian Healing*, Volume 17, #3, Fall, 1995, pp. 17-28.

space, and academe. A recent cover story in a national news magazine (Gibbs, 1995) reported the role prayer played in purportedly healing a little girl from a brain tumor. The same article quoted Christians claiming to gain ego strength by perceived interaction with God in prayer. In cyberspace *Christianity On-line* sponsors bulletin boards on which Christians post prayer requests for psychological and medical problems. Sometimes fellow Christians download these prayer requests and whole churches intercede for the petitioners. Also, on-line pamphlets cover theological issues such as the interrelationship between grace and prayer. Recently, the *American Psychologist* published a breakthrough article in which Jones (1994) argued that religion "could participate as an active partner with psychology as a science" (p. 184). A large part of this psychology/religion integration will include prayer.

Prayer has relevance to the subspecialty of behavioral medicine. A survey (Bearon and Koenig, 1990) of 40 adults (65-74 years) showed that mature people pray regularly for their health. Over half of the respondents reported praying for help and healing the last time they experienced a medical symptom. Respondents prayed most for serious symptoms which required medical attention. Results showed that prayer and medical treatment were not mutually exclusive. Further research suggests that praying with distressed patients is a therapeutic, mainstream activity. In a survey of family doctors from Illinois, Koenig, Lucille, and Dayringer (1989) found that many physicians pray with older patients and believe that it promotes health.

Relevant to the modern worldview and to health issues, prayer and prayer-like activities have been empirically investigated. This research is important to the mental health professional's understanding of prayer, but often important findings related to prayer go underreported. Benor (1992), a researcher and physician, found from a review of 150 studies of prayer and prayer-like techniques employed toward enzymes, plants, animals, and people that more than half of the scientific studies yielded significant results. Benor observed that if "healing were a medication, it would be on the market" (p. 74.)

A fuller understanding of prayer will enable psychologists to make this therapeutic behavior less professionally obscure and more available to clients. Awakened interest in prayer may generate innovations in Christian counseling. That the National Institute of Health awarded $28,800 in 1993 to study prayer interventions for substance abuse, suggests that a trend may already be underway (Health Responsibility Systems, Collective Work & Database, 1994).

This article represents an attempt to help mental health professionals further understand prayer and its psychological and biological effects on living systems. After first defining prayer from a Christian perspective, summaries of prayer studies relevant to mental health professionals, especially to practitioners of behavioral medicine, will be presented. This article also compiles

Christian prayer, as a psychological and behavioral medical intervention, enjoys empirical, anecdotal, and theoretical support as a means to influence human behavior and experience.

anecdotal and theoretical/theological observations germane to the prayer and its interface with psychology. The following sections argue from empirical data that prayer correlates with beneficial changes in physiological systems of people who pray, that prayers of a person or a group may influence the psychological and biological systems of others, and that prayer correlates with psychologically desirable states and outcomes. Over-all, this article provides an overview of prayer for interested mental health professionals and behavioral medicine specialists.

Psychotheological Aspects of Prayer

What is prayer? What is its nature and how is it defined? The nature of prayer differs across religions depending upon the conception of God. Christianity finds God essentially all-loving and all-powerful and revealed in Jesus Christ. Traditionally, Christian prayer is intimate communication with the benevolent deity (Finney and Malony, 1985). This intimate communication so varies, even from biblical times, that precisely defining prayer is difficult.

There is no one definition of prayer that will completely cover all references to it in the Bible. Prayer is often described in terms of intercourse and spiritual communion with God, with or without the mediation of priests or heavenly beings; it is usually, but not necessarily, vocal. By it the petitioner's will and activities are identified with God, effecting an intimate personal contact and relationship with Him (Masterman, 1967, p.669).

Working toward an understanding of prayer has occupied the church throughout the duration of its existence. According to the *New Catholic Encyclopedia* (1967) the Church's understanding of prayer developed through three epochs of church history: the patristic age, the scholastic age, and the modern age. In the patristic age, the church fathers conceived of prayer as "an appeal for good things made to God by devout people" and "a conversation and union between man and God" (p. 671). In the scholastic age theologians conceived of prayer often in terms of mere petition, asking for something without necessarily conversing. Most recently the understanding of prayer has broadened. In the wide sense the conception of prayer includes all prayer forms and emphasizes that the activity of prayer entails not only a monologue but a dialogue in which man relates to God, who has first related through His word and especially through the Word, Jesus, incarnate.

Throughout church epochs, the "conversation with God" in which Christian worshipers have engaged includes verbal prayers and mystical/contemplative prayers. Verbal prayer includes holy activities like petition, intercession, thanksgiving, and adoration. Mystical prayer, or contemplative prayer, can be defined as fully attending to God in a passive, nondefensive, nondemanding, open, nonverbal way. Contemplative prayer is not a technique; it is an interpersonal response to the Almighty. Contemplatives wait on God to deepen their confidence in his power and love so that they can grow in Christlikeness (Finney and Malony, 1985, p. 105).

According to the *Modern Catholic Encyclopedia* (Farrell, 1994) either verbal or contemplative prayer can be shaped by the needs, intentions, and attitudes that Christians bring to the activity of prayer. In verbal and nonverbal approaches to God, the worshiper often develops an internal posture and approaches the throne of grace with that stance. *Petition* is a form of prayer whereby the petitioner requests from God that God provide for personal needs or desires. God is asked to intervene so that the petitioner may receive their object. *Gratitude* is a prayer of thanks for the gifts bestowed by God. This prayer responds "to the wonders and joys of daily life by acknowledging and exhibiting appreciation to the one who has provided all" (p. 686). *Adoration* is the prayer that provides God with the devoted love, veneration, praise, and joyful submission that is due to God alone. *Reparation* is penitential prayer. It is prayer wherein one recognizes one's faults, feels sorrowful about them, and seeks reunion with God to further glorify Him.

Effects of Prayer and Prayer-Like
Interventions within Biological Systems

Clinical and research evidence indicates that some forms of prayer cause measurable, healthy changes in the organism, which in turn positively influence mental health. One form of prayer, recognized by Christian counselors (Kelsey, 1976) and behavior medicine specialists as particularly beneficial is the "Jesus Prayer" of Eastern Orthodoxy. Psychologically and medically beneficial, this prayer was recommended by St. Gregory Palamas, whose manuscript suggested that the Jesus Prayer should be conducted as follows:

Sit down alone and in silence. Lower your head, shut your eyes, breathe out gently, and imagine yourself looking into your own heart. As you breathe out say, "Lord Jesus Christ, have mercy on me." Say it moving your lips gently, or simply say it in your mind. Try to put all other thoughts aside. Be calm, be patient and repeat the process very frequently (from Benson, 1975 in Marcer, 1986, p. 23).

A fuller understanding of prayer will enable psychologists to make this therapeutic behavior less professionally obscure and more available to clients.

Of course, St. Gregory was neither a psychologist nor a medical researcher. He and his followers sought God. Yet, a by-product of the Jesus Prayer is holistic stress reduction, thus associating therapeutic as well as spiritual, efficacy with prayer.

> Gregory did not advise his followers to recite the Jesus Prayer in order to wean them off benzodiazapines or to cure their hypertension! He did so in order that they might have union with God [but] ... irrespective of its spiritual value, meditation has the power to combat a wide range of illnesses, especially those believed to be associated with stress. Much of the impetus for exploring the clinical application of meditation came from research into the relaxation response, which was conducted by Herbert Benson and his colleagues at the Harvard Medical School (Marcer, 1986, p. 23).

Benson conducted early research on Transcendental Meditation (TM), which in practice, although not in theology, much resembles the "Jesus Prayer." This research gave rise to considering the benefits of prayer and meditation as stress reduction tools. Repetitive prayers like the "Jesus Prayer" may benefit worshipers, because the spiritual practice reverses the "fight-or-flight" stress response.

The fight-or-flight response can adversely affect health. Grounded in evolutionary utility, the stress response causes involuntary, physiological changes when a person feels threatened. Unfortunately, the body responds to life threatening and non-life threatening stressors in much the same way. For example, an employee's body may respond to a non-life threatening boss' frown in the same way it would if confronted by a life threatening predatory animal. In either circumstance dramatic physical changes can occur. Confronted by a real or imagined threat, the hypothalamus activates the sympathetic nervous system to release adrenaline and noradrenaline. Once released into the soma, these messengers create an aroused state (Benson and Stuart, 1992).

Continual arousal in the face of marginal threats menaces heath because of the taxing psychosomatics involved. Metabolism, heart rate, blood pressure, breathing rate, and muscle tension all increase. Prolonged over time, the stress response creates physical problems like hypertension, heart trouble, headaches, digestive and stomach anomalies and lowered immunity. The stress response also correlates with psychological problems like anxiety, panic, pessimism, and so forth.

Problems associated with stress led researchers to look for a stress anti-dote. Benson found that the body possesses the capacity to counter-balance the stress response with a relaxation response. During the relaxation re-sponse markers of psychological stress reverse. Heart rate drops, breathing rate drops, and so forth. All of this has been scientifically documented. Re-search into TM showed that meditation can reverse the stress response and trigger the relaxation response. Clinical evidence gathered by Benson and his colleagues at the Mind/Body Institute further suggests that repetitive Christian prayer triggers the relaxation response (Benson and Stuart, 1992). Their case studies report abatement of stress-related physical problems, as well as lessened anxiety, freedom from worry, and reduced negativism. At the same time, self-esteem increases among repetitive prayer practitioners, characterized by a sense of improved performance and efficiency.

Furthermore, a recent study into the health/spirituality relationship con-ducted by Benson's colleague, Jared Kass, Ph.D. at Boston's Deaconess Hospital:

> … found that a significant number of those who elicit the relaxation response ... reported an increase in positive attitudes associated with spirituality. Spirituality in this study was linked to increased life pur-pose and satisfaction. They also found that an increase in positive atti-tudes contributed to improvements in health. (Benson and Stuart, 1992, p. 38).

In summary, repetitive prayer and prayer-like activities appear to trigger mechanisms associated with the relaxation response and correlates with positive attitudes and good health.[1]

In *The Wellness Book* (1992) Benson advises that two components are required to elicit the relaxation response, (a) a mental focusing device like a repetitive prayer, word, or sound, and (b) a passive attitude toward distract-ing thoughts, directing the mind back to the prayer when clients become conscious of straying into a train of thought. His instructions for eliciting the relaxation response sound like the writing of an updated St. Gregory:

> (a) Pick a focus word, phrase, image or prayer. It can be rooted in your personal belief system. For example a Christian might choose the open-ing of Psalm 23, *the Lord is my shepherd ....* (b) Sit quietly in a com-fortable position. (c) Close your eyes. (d) Relax your muscles. (e) Breathe slowly and naturally, and as you do, repeat your focus word or phrase as you exhale. (f) Assume a passive attitude. Do not worry about how well you are doing. When other thoughts come to mind,

Clinical and research evidence indicates that some forms of prayer cause measurable, healthy changes in the organism, which in turn positively influence mental health.

simply say to yourself, "Oh well," and gently return to the repetition. (g) Continue for ten or twenty minutes. (h) Practice the technique once or twice daily. (Benson and Stuart, 1992, p. 46).

Benson recommends utilizing the technique in the morning and in the evening for twenty minutes each time. The location should be relatively free from distractions. While relaxing the worshiper should assume a comfortable position, kneeling or sitting with relaxed muscles. Often, while eliciting the relaxation response through prayer, worshipers find it useful to breathe deeply, coordinating their prayer with their breath. Additionally, clinical evidence shows that combining faith with repetition of prayer words increases the likelihood that beneficial psychophysiological effects of the relaxation response will occur. Prayers that Christians find beneficial in the clinical setting include "Come, Lord," "Lord, have mercy," "Our Father," "Our Father who art in heaven," "Lord Jesus Christ, have mercy on me," "Hail Mary," and "The Lord is my shepherd" (Benson and Stuart, 1992, p. 51). Benson found that practices of this sort globally impact a person's life. As prayer elicits the relaxation response, a person tends to carry the physiologically based sense of peace into everyday life.

Some medical experts agree with Benson that prayer, along with other relaxation producing techniques, improves health. Hall and O'Grady (1991) remark in *Psychoneuroimmunology* that

> ... interventions that are thought by some to have health promoting effects include guided imagery, biofeedback, *prayer* as well as the common denominator in all these strategies, relaxation. Recent studies suggest that these types of interventions may be capable of altering the immunocompetence of the individual (p. 1068).

While medical experts like Benson, Hall and O'Grady advance the idea that prayer is a factor in health improvement, literature searches reveal little direct experimental evidence that changes occur in the relaxed bodies of those who pray. Benson and his colleagues based his inferences that repetitive prayer triggers the relaxation response from their TM studies and uncontrolled clinical evidence. Similarly, Hall and O'Grady have lumped prayer with relaxation in general which is proven to enhance immunity (Masters, Burish, Hollon, and Rimm, 1987). Hence, their association of prayer with immuno-enhancing relaxation strategies is inferential. Perhaps future research will strengthen and factualize these reasonable assertions.[2]

One study, however, did find positive measurable bodily changes in praying Christians. Surwillo and Hobson (1978) were interested to see if EEG's of praying Christians would show the same slowing of brain waves found in average Transcendental Mediators. They selected six subjects from the evangelical, Protestant Church of God, chosen because of their devout religious life. Subjects devoted an average of 30 minutes a day to prayer, some praying up to an hour. During the experiment, subject's EEG's were taken at rest before prayer, during prayer, and after prayer. Prayer itself consisted mostly of adoration and praise of God. Contrary to the hypothesis, brain waves of these advanced worshipers actually increased during 20 minute prayer conditions. "From this standpoint, it would appear that the individual's state of consciousness during prayer is quite different from that reported to occur during Transcendental Meditation" (p. 140). Accounting for this, the investigators observed that advanced Transcendental Meditation and advanced yogic meditation have produced similar high-frequency brain wave activity among adepts. They suggested that

> ... highly experienced meditators—persons who would be considered "masters"—may show an acceleration in frequency of electrocortical activity, particularly during deep meditation. The similarity of these results to those obtained in the present investigation from subjects during prayer is striking indeed. (p. 142).

Anecdotally, a subject in the study whose brain waves shifted the most during prayer also exhibited the most devout behavior outside of the laboratory in her everyday lifestyle. Getting up at 5 a.m. daily, she prayed for at least an hour, reportedly with tears flowing freely down her cheeks. Although the very small number of research subjects in this study precludes generalization or even definitive interpretation, the results are suggestive that devout Christian prayer can dramatically and measurably affect the body.

Prayer Within Human and Nonhuman Biological Systems
Despite limited scientific evidence that prayer for others improves their health, people continue to pray recovery from illness and believe that it benefits their health. A recent survey of cystic fibrosis patients and their families (Stern, Cana, and Doershuk, 1992) revealed that among the most common non-medical therapies utilized by respondents, patients and their families overwhelmingly was to seek out groups of people to pray for them. Survey data indicated that respondents perceived group prayer to increase their or their loved-one's health and to provide psychosocial benefits. Group prayer was the most common nonmedical therapy (48%); of these, 65% used

...a by-product of the Jesus Prayer is holistic stress reduction, thus associating therapeutic as well as spiritual, efficacy with prayer.

group prayer frequently, and 93% perceived benefit (primarily maintaining health in asymptomatic patients). In addition, group prayer reportedly benefited patient/family members by demonstrating family/community support. The fact that 93% perceived benefit when others pray for them is an important finding. The mere fact that people believe that others' prayers improve their health makes the matter worthy of further research. Two studies have looked at prayer's effects on humans.

Collipp (1969, in Dossey, 1993) conducted a small study on the effect of prayer on a group of children with leukemia and compared outcomes to a group of children in a no-prayer control group. The names of 10 out of 18 leukemic children were randomly selected and sent to individuals who had agreed to organize a prayer group. Ten families were enlisted in their Protestant Church to pray daily for these 10 children. They were not told that this was a study on the efficacy of prayer. Each family received weekly reminders of its obligation. The 10 Protestant families prayed for the 10 children in the experiment group for 15 months. The results were startling: "Of 10 children with leukemia in the experimental group 7 were still alive; of 8 children with leukemia in the control group, only 2 were alive" (p. 202). The difference in survival was at the 90% level of significance. Collipp concluded that the data supported the hypothesis that Christian prayers for the sick are efficacious. However, a less enthusiastic Dossey (1993) criticized the experiment for having too few research subjects—compromising generalizability of findings, no checks on the people praying were made (to see if they in fact prayed), and diagnostic dissimilarities between prayer and control groups made true comparison between groups difficult.

Another, better controlled, study concerned the impact of prayer upon coronary patients. A cardiologist, Byrd (1988) designed and implemented a now classic study at the coronary care unit of San Francisco General Hospital. Over ten months, 393 patients admitted to a hospital coronary care unit for heart attack. Patients were assigned randomly to either an intercessory prayer group (IP) or a no prayer group (NP) control condition. Christians prayed for the IP group from outside the hospital. The NP group received no prayer. Patients and hospital staff were blind to which patients were in which group. At the study's finish, the prayed-for group were five times less likely to need antibiotics than no-prayer counterparts. Also, prayed-for patients had significantly less pulmonary edema (a heart related lung problem) than no-prayer patients. Prayed-for patients were intubated (artificially ventilated) less often than no-prayer patients; and fewer people in the prayed-for group died, although the result was not statistically significant. Byrd (1988) wrote, "These data suggest that intercessory prayer to the Judeo-Christian God has a beneficial therapeutic effect in patients admitted to a coronary care unit" (p. 826).[3]

While more research is needed to empirically establish the efficacy of people praying for one another, one group of Christian researchers have begun to establish that prayer in fact contributes to health of non-human biological systems. Spindrift is an organization of Christian parapsychologists who evaluated the effects of prayer on unlikely research subjects, usually beans, sprouts, yeast, and so forth. They have found that prayer actually does have a measurable biological effect on living physical systems. For example, one Spindrift researcher, Fairfax (1993), reported findings of bean experiments to show that prayer influences the capacity of beans to hydrate. Results further showed that beans tended to sprout more if they had been prayed for, and that mental proximity to beans in the minds of those praying influenced the weight gain of beans. Spindrift (1993) asserts that such experiments have scientific credibility and that some of their work has received partial endorsement by Ph.D.s conversant in experimental work. This last assertion, however, was published by Spindrift itself and no names were given; hence, we have no way to judge whether truly qualified experts have independently endorsed their research. A literature review has found only Dossey addressing Spindrift's work.

Dossey (1993), an ecumenically oriented authority on prayer research, has given credence to Spindrift's Christian prayer research. In *Healing Words* (1993) Dossey suggests that Spindrift's research into the impact of prayer on biological systems sheds light on how exactly Christian prayer (and prayer in general) might be most effective.

> The Spindrift organization ... has performed simple laboratory experiments showing that prayer works. After proving that prayer is effective, they proceeded to investigate which type of prayer strategy works best. One of their most important contributions is the distinction they make between *directed* and *nondirected* prayer. Practitioners of directed prayer have a specific goal, image, or outcome in mind. They are "directing" the system, attempting to steer it in a precise direction. They may be praying for the cancer to be cured, the heart attack to resolve itself, or the pain to go away. Nondirected prayer, in contrast, is an open-ended approach in which no specific outcome is held in mind. In nondirected prayer the practitioner does not attempt to tell the universe [or, in the Christian's case, God] what to do (p. 97).

For Dossey, the prayer principle drawn from Spindrift experiments corroborates a biblical principle. "One need only pray for what's best - the 'Thy will be done' approach" (p. 100). In the Lord's prayer, prescribed by Jesus to his disciples, this approach of surrendering the individual, directive will to God, while adapting an agendaless, nondirective approach to prayer is implicit in Jesus' words: "... your will be done on earth as it is in heaven" (Mt 6:10). God appears to work through our prayer intentions in the most perfect, healing way, if we remove our specific requirements from the prayer.

The Spindrift research begins to establish that Christian prayer can cause measurable differences in targeted biological systems. It further suggests that the mechanism of healing action, whether God or grace, may best be unleashed when we pray nondirectively, praying, "Thy will be done."

Psychological Effects of Prayer

Anecdotal and empirical evidence suggests that a relationship exists between prayer and psychological healing. A Jesuit priest (Dunn, 1981) recorded highlights of an interview with a 55 year old woman who felt that prayers for healing her low self-esteem had been answered.

> She talked about how for years she had wearied herself with analyzing, hitting at symptoms but never striking the root. "It came with a bang. I still have problems, but I'm one with myself now. I'm satisfied to stay in the present, and I'm not always anxious about the future and the past. I feel as though I have finally fallen into my niche. I can handle my problems with confidence." I asked her whether this [healing and answer to prayer] was when she really found God. Surprisingly, she said No. "I have been at one with God in my deepest being," she said, "but not in my psychology. Then that part of me, too, joined that deeper part of me where I am one with God" (p. 37).

This woman experienced inner healing. Is there any research evidence to corroborate her experience that prayer influences psychological health?

One study used frontalis muscle tension (electromyograph—EMG) and anxiety measures to research prayer's impact on anxiety. Elkins, Anchor, and Sandler (1979) compared frontalis muscle tension and results of anxiety measures across a prayer (either intercessory or reflective) group, a relaxation training group, and a control group.

> Group comparisons on EMG readings revealed that ... prayer produced less tension reduction than relaxation training but only slightly (non) significant more tension reduction than the control condition. On [anxiety measures], this same between group relationship was found with the prayer group's rated anxiety reduction barely failing to be statistically significant as compared to the control group. This finding suggests that prayer group subjects tended to experience a greater amount

of tension reduction as a result of prayer than actually was measured physiologically (p. 86).

In other words, the prayer group experienced less muscle relaxation than the relaxation training group but the prayer group did (although not statistically significant) relax more than controls. In this study, prayer tended to reduce psychophysiologically measured anxiety. While not statistically significant, the results suggest that under certain conditions prayer positively reduces anxiety.

In another study, Carlson, Bacaseta, and Simanton (1988) compared psychological and physiological outcomes across a devotional meditation (DM) or devotional prayer group, progressive relaxation (PR), and wait-list control (WL) group. While measured for frontalis muscle tension and skin temperature, the DM group sat quietly, then listened to taped scriptural material, reflected upon it for two minutes in silence, engaged in liturgical prayer, and reflected again. DM sessions lasted 20 minutes. The results of the study were promising for DM-style prayer. As operationalized above, DM changes

... several psychological and physiological variables in a population of Christian students. Following a 2-week program where subjects individually were exposed to DM, it was found that they reported less anger and anxiety than persons who underwent 2 weeks of PR training or who were assigned to a wait-list control group. Furthermore, persons experiencing DM also displayed less muscle tension, as measured by reduced EMG activity ... than did persons who performed PR ... the present results offer strong support for continued exploration of the efficacy of DM strategies for reducing clinically relevant symptoms among persons with a Christian background (p. 366).

A famous study of psychological effects of prayer (Parker and St. Johns, 1957) involved assigning 45 psychotherapy clients to nine months of either weekly individual psychotherapy, daily individual home prayer, or weekly structured group prayer. Symptoms across the three groups included anxiety, depression, anger, and somatic complaints. At the end of the nine months self-report and psychological testing showed 72% reported improvement in the structured prayer therapy group, 65% improvement in the psychotherapy group, and no improvement in the home prayer group. Commenting on their data, Parker and St. Johns noted that psychotherapy worked well, but not as well as group prayer, because while learning more adaptive and honest psychological stances, the clients did not have a curative connection to the divine. They went on to say that the group of individuals that prayed at home, those in the individual home prayer group, may have prayed in maladaptive ways that reinforced their problems. An example of a minister's son illus-

... psychotherapy worked well, but not as well as group prayer, because while learning more adaptive and honest psychological stances, the clients did not have a curative connection to the divine.

trates this point.

> Jerry ... used rote prayer ... reiterated his guilt and his "wormy" feelings, constantly asking for forgiveness which he never took. His concept of God was a faraway Being which increased his feelings of dependence and inadequacy because he could never be sure He was Listening. Each night he confirmed his symptoms, his discontent, his hopelessness, following this with a positive statement that he was not worthy of anything better, and for 271 evenings straight he told God and himself what a failure they made as a team (p. 50).

Ultimately, the researchers concluded that the prayer group succeeded, because it drew upon psychological insights drawn from psychological testing and group feedback, allowing the members to pray honestly about real problems in the supportive context of a curatively minded group that prayed proactively. Following weekly two hour group sessions, each prayer group participant had prayer homework.

> Four guidelines were given for this prayer. First of all, it had to be regular. Secondly, it had to be an act of surrender. The individual was to pray with the attitude of giving up his or her desires and demands, seeking only to do God's will. Thirdly, the prayers were to be positive, affirmative statements rather than desperate begging or negative statements. While praying, the subjects were to visualize themselves as they desired themselves to be. Finally, the prayer was to be receptive. Participants in the prayer therapy were asked to pray believing that they had already received what they requested from God (Finney and Malony, 1985, p. 108).

Unfortunately, the experiment was poorly controlled. No control group existed, psychometric assessment may have been unreliable, and extraneous variables were not taken into account. Nevertheless, this study represented an indication that prayer may be psychologically beneficial under the right circumstances.

Still other studies of prayer and psychology have been accomplished. Research by Welford (1947), positively reviewed by Finney and Malony (1985), suggests that the motivation to pray in a petitionary manner stems from the need to reduce frustrations and the need to come to terms with unusual situations. The conclusion is that petitionary prayer may be a positive means of adjustment that reflects Christian metaphysical assumptions. A study on the effects of verbal prayer by Carson and Huss (1979) cited Finney and Malony (1985), compared two groups of chronic undifferentiated schizophrenics, the experimental group incorporating prayers about the love of God and the worth of each individual into ten weekly meetings with nursing students. The control group received only a therapeutic relationship. Psychological measures showed that.

> ... the experimental group grew in their ability to express anger and aggression. They also became more hopeful about changing their lives, exhibited more appropriate affect, and decreased in somatic complaints (Finney and Malony, 1985, p. 110).

Finney and Malony (1985) found that flaws in the study's design make the results merely suggestive.

Two studies on contemplative prayer (Mallory, 1977 and Sacks, 1979, both in Finney and Malony, 1985) suggest that contemplative prayer among Catholic religious populations is associated with positive mental health and cognitive integration. Unfortunately, one study had methodological problems; the other had results that only tended toward significance.

Morgan (1983) found frequent prayer impacts object relations, i.e. frequent prayer is associated with being nice to others. From the point of view of the psychology of religion this makes sense. If a person relates to God in an open and honest way while subscribing to Christian principles, they may be disposed to relate to others in the same generous, graceful way in which they experience God in prayer. Using survey data, Morgan (1983) established a strong connection between frequent prayer and positive behaviors toward others.

> Those who pray frequently, those who have integrated prayer into day-to-day life, seem to practice what they preach. The prayerful are less likely to intensely dislike anyone, to feel resentful when they don't get their way, to like to gossip or to get very angry or upset .... On the other hand, the more prayerful are more likely to stop and comfort a crying child, to be a good listener, and even to get along with loud mouthed obnoxious people. [Prayerful people] apparently turn the other cheek too, because they do these things despite the fact that they are no more likely to consider their fellow man/woman fair, helpful, or trustworthy than the less prayerful. Finally, ... in the interview situation ... interviewers judged the more prayerful as more cooperative and friendly. Are religious people nice people? ... yes—prayerful people do seem

"Prayer makes the virtue of ... charity more vital and dynamic in a person's life."

more friendly and cooperative (pp. 690-691).

According to the *New Catholic Encyclopedia* (1967) "Prayer makes the virtue of ... charity more vital and dynamic in a person's life" (p. 671). Morgan's conclusions corroborate this claim. Morgan's along with other studies mentioned here suggest that prayer measurably influences emotional health and psychologically determined factors like object relations.

Conclusions

Relevant to the modern American Christian, prayer appears to factor in as an important aspect of the modern worldview and behavioral practice. Research and anecdotal evidence creates an incomplete but growing argument that prayer positively influences the psychology and psycho-physiology of those for whom the prayers are offered. On similar lines, anecdotal and research evidence exists which paves the way for establishing that prayer by a person or group may influence targeted biological systems. Other research and anecdotal evidence raises the question whether or not prayer plays a role in determining emotional health and positive object relations. These findings suggest that Christian therapists wishing to incorporate prayer into the therapeutic process should familiarize themselves with psychobiological and psychotheological aspects of prayer. Further developments in clinical practice and empirical research may prove that prayer contributes to increased health and wholeness of the individual.

Reference Notes

1. Researches at the University of Pennsylvania (Newberg, et. al., 2001) studied a small group of Tibetan Buddhist and Roman Catholic nuns. The Buddhists meditated and the nuns practiced Centering Prayer. Observed via brain imaging technology, subjects' brains changed dramatically and nonpathologically while they enjoyed a sense of freedom from self and merged with the Ultimate. This brain imaging study of the praying brain has inaugurated the field of neurotheology. Eventually, such research will further our understanding of the neurological underpinnings of the health benefits of mystical Christian prayer. The most healthful aspect of such prayer, however, is least easy to measure, which is the love that supplicants and God enjoy in their intimate communion.
2. Newly reviewed research (Seeman, et. al., 2003) bears out that meditation and prayer techniques bless the body. Well designed studies show that meditation appears to lower blood pressure (Sneider, et. al., 1995), correlates with lower cholesterol levels (Patel, et. al., 1985), and is associated with improved health

outcomes in clinical patient populations (Kabat-Zinn, et. al., 1998). Many of the studied meditation/prayer practices have been "baptized" and fruitfully employed by various Christian faith communities.

3.   In 1999 Harris replicated the Byrd study with a larger sample size (n=990) that generated remarkably similar results. Scientific evidence mounts that prayer will foster recovery from heart attacks.

References

Bearon, L. and Koenig, H (1990). Religious cognitions and use of prayer in health and illness. *The Gerontologist*, 30, 2 249-253.

Benor, D. (1992). Lessons from spiritual healing research & practice. *Subtle Energies*, 3, 73-88.

Benson, H. (1975). *The relaxation response.* New York: William Marrow.

Benson, H. and Stuart, E. (Eds.). (1992). *The wellness book: The comprehensive guide to maintaining health and treating stress-related illness.* New York: Birch Lane Press.

Byrd, R. (1988). Positive therapeutic effects of intercessory prayer in a coronary care unit population. *Southern Medical Journal*, 81, 826-829.

Carlson, C. Bacaseta, P. and Simanton, D. (1988). A controlled evaluation of devotional meditation and progressive relaxation. *Journal of Psychology and Theology*, 16, 362-368.

Carson, V. and Huss, K. (1979). Prayer, an effective therapeutic and teaching tool. *Journal of Psychiatric Nursing*, 17, 34-37.

Collipp, P. (1969). The efficacy of prayer. *Medical Times*, 97, 5, 201-204.

Dossey, L. (1993). *Healing words: The power of prayer and the practice of medicine.* San Francisco: Harper.

Dunn, T. (1981). *We cannot find words.* Denville, NJ: Dimension Books.

Elkins, D. Anchor, K. and Sandler, H. (1979). Relaxation training and prayer behavior as tension reduction techniques. *Behavioral Engineering, 5*, 81-87.

Fairfax, S. (1993). The world of thought: Its four ratios, as seen in tests with germinating seeds. *The spindrift papers.* (Spindrift, Inc., Ed.) Vol. 1, 1975-1993. Ft. Lauderdale, Fl: Spindrift, Inc.

Farrell, E (1994). Prayer. *The Modern Catholic Encyclopedia* (M. Glazier & M. Hellig, Eds.). Collegeville, MN: The Liturgical Press.

Finney, J. and Malony, N. (1985). Empirical studies of christian prayer. *Journal of Psychology and Theology*, 13, 104-115.

Gibbs, N. (1995). The message of miracles. *Time* (Accessed through America On-Line, April 8, 1995).

Greeley, A. (1991). Keeping the faith: Americans hold fast to the rock of ages. *Omni*, 13,11,6.

Hall, N. and O'Grady, M. (1991) *Psychoneuroimmunology.* (R. Ader, D. Felton, and N. Cohen, Eds.). (2nd ed.). San Diego: Academic Press, Inc.

Harris, W., Gowda, M., Kolb, J., Strychacz, C. Bacek, J., and Jones, P. (1999). A randomized, controlled trial of the effects of remote, intercessory prayer on outcomes in patients admitted to the coronary care unit. *Archives of Internal Medicine, 159*, 2273-2278.

Health Responsibility Systems, Collective work & Database (1994). NIH grants:

therapies, illnesses (Database accessed through America On-Line and cites the following as source: US Department of Health & Human Services, National Institutes of Health, Office of Alternative Medicine, 1, 2, November 1993)

Henning, G. (1981). An analysis of perceived positive and negative prayer outcomes. *Journal of Psychology and Theology*, 9, 352-358.

Jones, S. L. (1994). A constructive relationship for religion with the science and profession of psychology. *The American Psychologist, 19,* 184-199.

Kabat-Zinn, J., Wheeler, E., Light, T., Skillinos, A., Scharf, M., and Cropley, T. (1998). Influence of a mindfulness meditation-based stress reduction intervention on rates of skin clearing in patients with moderate to severe psoriasis undergoing phototherapy (UVB) and photochemotherapy (PUVA). *Psychosomatic Medicine, 60*, 625-632.

Keating, T. (1994). *Intimacy with god.* New York: Crossroad.

Kelsey, M. (1976). *The other side of silence: A guide to Christian meditation.* New York: Paulist Press.

Koenig, H. Lucille, B. and Dayringer, R. (1989). Physician perspectives on the role of religion in the physician—older patient relationship. *The Journal of Family Practice*, 28, 441-448.

Mallory, M. (1977). *Christian mysticism: Transcending techniques.* Amsterdam: Van Gorcum Assen.

Marcer, D. (1986). *Biofeedback and related therapies in clinical practice.* Rockville, MD: Aspen Publishers, Inc.

Martin, J. and Carlson, C. (1988). Spiritual dimensions of health psychology. *Behavior therapy and religion* (W. Miller and J. Martin, Eds.). Beverly Hills: SAGE Publications.

Masterman, M. (1967). Prayer in the bible. *New Catholic Encyclopedia* (Editorial staff at the Catholic University of America, Eds.). Vol. 4. Planatine, IL: Jack Heraty & Associates.

Masters, J. Burish, T. Hollon, S. and Rimm, D. (1987). *Behavior therapy: techniques and empirical findings* (3rd ed.). New York: Harcourt Brace Jovanovich College Publishers.

Morgan, S. (1983). A research note on religion and morality: Are religious people nice people? *Social Forces*, 61, 683-692.

New Catholic Encyclopedia (1967). Prayer (theology of). *New Catholic Encyclopedia.* (Editorial staff at the Catholic University of America, Eds.). Vol. *11.* Planatine,IL: Jack Heraty & Associates.

Newberg, A., D'Aquili, E., and Rause, V. (2001). *Why god won't go away.* New York: Ballentine.

Parker, W. and St. Johns E. (1957). *Prayer can change your life: Experiments and techniques in prayer therapy.* Carmel, NY: Guideposts.

Patel, C., Marmont, M., Terry, D., Carruthers, M. Hunt, B., and Patel, M. (1985). Trial of relaxation in reducing coronary risk: Four year follow up. *British Medical Journal, 290*, 1103-1106.

Sacks, H. (1979). The effect of spiritual exercises on the integration of the self-system. *Journal for the Scientific Study of Religion*, 18, 46-50.

Schneider, R., Staggers, F., Alexander, C., Sheppard, W., Rainforth, M. and Kondwani, K. (1995). A randomized controlled trial of stress reduction for hypertension in older African Americans. *Hypertension, 26*, 820-827.

Seeman, T., Dubin, L. and Seeman, M. (2003). Religiosity/spirituality and health: A critical review of the evidence for biological pathways. *American Psychologist, 58*, 53-63.

Spindrift, Inc. (Ed.) (1993). *The Spindrift papers.* Vol. 1, 1975-1993. Ft. Lauderdale, FL: Spindrift, Inc.

Stern, R. Cana, E. and Doershuk, C. (1992). Use of nonmedical treatment by cystic fibrosis patients. *Journal of Adolescent Health*, 13, 612-615.

Surwillo, W. and Hobson, D. (1978). Brain electrical activity during prayer. *Psychological Reports*, 43, 135-143.

Wallace, R. and Benson, H. (1972). The physiology of meditation. *Scientific American,* 226, 2.

Welford, A. (1947). Is religious behavior dependent upon affect or frustration? *Journal of Abnormal and Social Psychology*, 42, 310-319.

Ron Pekala, Ph.D. is an authority on behavioral medicine, hypnosis, and phenomenology. His practice includes both hospital and private work. He is an Adjunct Professor in the Doctor of Psychology Program at Immaculata College.

The Societal, Clinical, and Medical Necessity for the Church to Restore Her Healing Ministry *

Charles L. Zeiders, Psy.D. and Veruschka DeMarici, Psy.D.

The authors propose that the church should aggressively reinvigorate her healing ministry. It is believed that healing of persons will culminate in evangelism. Societal, clinical, and medical reasons necessitating the increase of the healing ministry are discussed. It is argued that the healing ministry is legitimized by scripture, tradition, and reason. This article is based upon a paper that the authors presented to the Archdiocese of Philadelphia.

A s Christian clinicians, we have become aware of the great need for the church to reassert her ministry of healing in the power of the Holy Spirit. We have developed a three-fold vision of the healing ministry and have analyzed societal, clinical, and medical trends that recommend the urgent need for the church to aggressively increase the healing ministry. It is our contention that the healing ministry remains supported by scripture, tradition, and reason. Nothing should impede this way of imitating Jesus Christ.

Components of the Healing Vision

The vision has three components that culminate in evangelism: (1) Priests and many lay persons are gifted with the tremendous healing power that the Holy Spirit has made available since the time of Our Lord. The great spiritual genius, St. Paul, tells us that these spiritual gifts come to the church through the pleasure of the Holy Spirit and that this gifting is to be used for the general good of the people (1 Cor. 12: 4-11). (2) Persons still need healing. Luke tells us that the crowds flocked to Jesus, because he made such beautiful healing available to them. The people came to him "to be cured of their diseases. Persons tormented by unclean spirits were also cured and everyone in the crowd was trying to touch him, because power came out of him and cured them all" (Lk. 6:18-19). Today, as in the first century, broken humanity yearns for divine healing. (3) As persons heal, the gospel will be demonstrated. People will realize that their God and their church are proactive, relevant, and excitingly kind. The healed will tell others how God has

---

* This article was first published in *The Journal of Christian Healing*, Volume 20, #3&4, Fall/Winter, 1998, pp. 30-36.

People will realize that their God and their church are proactive, relevant, and excitingly kind.

healed them, and some will pray for the sick who will be healed and motivated for deeper conversion. As this dynamic increases, the population at large will become curious and spiritually aroused to investigate the church. In this way, the healing ministry will "proclaim the gospel to all creation" (Mk. 16:16), as Our Lord commanded us to do for the glory of God and the salvation of souls.

The Urgency for Healing
Societal, clinical, and medical factors point to the urgency for the church to aggressively pursue her healing ministry.

Societal Reasons
Societal reasons involve the fact that people are religiously minded without having Christian religious training. While people are as religious as ever, they are less and less "churched," making them vulnerable to harmful occult influences. Evidence that people are still religious is based on polls that show:

- 82% of polled people pray for health or success
- 75% pray for strength to overcome personal weakness
- 87% say that God answers prayers
- 29% pray to God more than 1x a day
- 25% pray 1x a day
- 79% believe that God answers prayers for healing someone with an incurable illness
- 73% think that God answers prayers for help in finding a job (Woodward,1997)

Further,

> ...80% of Americans - of various religious faiths and of none - say they believe in life after death, and two thirds are certain there is a heaven. This may be explained by the religious nature of society today. By almost every measure, the United States is a nation steeped in religion, more so than all other Western nations except Poland and Ireland (Sheler, 1997).

Various other polls show conclusively that Americans maintain religious practices and beliefs in large numbers.

Clinical Reasons

As practicing psychotherapists, we have come to appreciate that the core of psychopathology is the absence of love. We believe that the church has the doctrinal, sacramental, and spiritual armaments best suited to attack the core of psychopathology. We further believe that the Holy Spirit is real and, when experienced, is recognized immediately by patients as a healing presence more natively satisfying than any other healing attempt or experience.

Much psychopathology has a spiritual component best treated within a Christian context. For instance, the church has always recognized that doing what is morally good is always therapeutic. Psychology and psychiatry need to learn this from the church and the church can educate them simply by continuing to operate from this timeless principle.

Many young Christians have fallen away from the faith and have become wounded as the result of engaging in behaviors consistent with the postmodern *Zeitgeist*. In therapy we find a preponderance of Christians in their twenties who are devastated from abortions, drug use, illicit relationships, and occult involvement. We need to be able to refer them to appropriate, loving, healing authorities.

Our clinical experience and scholarly research indicate to us that Christian prayer is effective in healing both psychological and somatic disorders. While we will not cease from praying for our clients nor advocating that other care providers do the same, there is no substitute for a church that is fully grounded in her healing ministry to accomplish healings in Christ's name.

Medical Reasons

The emergence of alternative medicine is another reason that points to the urgency of the church's need to advance her healing ministry. Alternative medicine includes healing treatments not generally found in mainstream medical schools or psychology programs. The field includes aromatherapy, color healing, light healing, sound healing, reflexology, acupuncture, energy medicine, and meditation.

Important thinkers in this field have gained credibility among care givers as a result of their scientific research. They have then gone on to advocate religious practices and doctrines which they treat as technical advances over orthodox Christianity.

Of concern is the emerging field of psychoneuroimmunology. This field studies and applies ways that the mind and body interact, causing health and illness. Researchers have convincingly shown that constant arousal tends to cause a variety of stress-related disorders like degraded immunity and cardiovascular problems. To intervene psychoneuroimmunologists urge physicians and psychologists to teach their patients ways to trigger the relaxation response. The relaxation response is a mental and physiological state oppo-

In therapy we find a preponderance of Christians in their twenties who are devastated from abortions, drug use, illicit relationships, and occult involvement. We need to be able to refer them to appropriate, loving, healing authorities.

site to the fight/flight response. It is characterized by psychosomatic calm and long-term health benefits. In and of itself this new medical field is spiritually innocuous—no better or worse than an antibiotic. Many of its proponents, however, advance a spirituality that in practice amounts to syncretism. Because many of these health-care providers are not churched, they train their patients to enter relaxed states, often induced by non—Christian meditation techniques like TM or mindfulness meditation.

A need exists for the church to take a leadership role in educating persons that all the benefits of the relaxation response are available without putting them in spiritual peril via occult practices. The rosary, the Jesus prayer, and other Christian contemplative techniques are psychoneuroimmunologically beneficial, while pointing the people away from antichrist and toward the Holy Physician.

Other Reasons

The Holy Spirit has ministered healing from the first century to the present. In the present era, the age of science, the church—if led by the Spirit—stands poised not only to continue her healing mission, but also to inform the scientific community about the nature and means of true healing. A look at the early church, church history, and the present scientific age show that God has always healed and offers the possibility of more healing and a fuller understanding of its nature.

The Gospels are full of Jesus' healing stories. The Book of *Acts* shows the Apostles healing a variety of illnesses in a variety of contexts. And the epistles show the apostles explicitly advancing the idea that the Holy Spirit gifts the church with healing (e.g. I Corinthians 12:7-11), and provides practical "how to" advice to those who need to avail themselves of the healing grace which flows from the Spirit of Jesus Christ (e.g. James 5:13-16, recommending prayer of faith, oil, confession). Scripture supports the healing ministry.

Church history abounds with stories of people healing in Christ's name. It is known that Church Fathers from Justin Martyr (AD 165) to Clement (AD 275), important Christian thinkers recognized healing as a function that the Church exercises in the Holy Spirit. Augustine came to recognize that God heals prior to his death in AD 430. St. Patrick (AD 461) healed the blind. St. Bernard (AD 1008) healed the lame, the dumb, and the deaf. Edward the

Confessor (AD 1042) healed scrofula. Valentine Greatrakes (AD 1600's) healed epilepsy, pain, and fever though the laying on of hands and praying. Following W.W.II, a revival in healing came upon the church. Katherine Kuhlman, Agnes Sanford, and Francis and Judith MacNutt have all been leaders in this regard. Tradition supports the healing ministry.

Social and medical science has begun to demonstrate the positive relationship between religious and spiritual practices and human well being. While the 1994 *Catechism of the Catholic Church* cautions that science by itself "cannot disclose the meaning of existence and of human progress" (p. 611) science increasingly demonstrates to the church her importance in the maintenance of health. For example, a review of more than a decade of research published in two leading psychiatry journals by the National Institute for Healthcare Research found that religion had a positive impact on clinical results very much of the time (Matthews, Larson & Barry, 1993). Encouraged by this positive outcome data, the church can suggest to the health-care community the true mechanism of action through which the measured health of her children is preserved. The church can instruct the community of health scientists that the positive outcome data on measures of well-being points human reason to the fact that the blessed Trinity is the author of human health. Positive outcome data is a measured, outward expression of our ultimate health in Jesus Christ. It represents a data point in the argument that the church has the authority to heal the children of God. Reason supports the church's healing ministry.

The Problem

At the Harvard Medical School's conference entitled *Spirituality and Healing in Medicine II*, held in Boston from December 15-12, 1996, George Gallop cautioned that, while survey data demonstrates high spirituality among Americans, "there is clear evidence that religion of faith is often not very deep." We believe that spirituality without religious training and Christian spiritual fail-safes has allowed people to engage in practices that are harmful to them in body, mind, and spirit. Examples include channeling, spiritism, past life regression, pagan meditation practices, hallucinogenic drugs, nature religions, angel worship, and so forth.

Since our society is very religious but less grounded in orthodox faith than ever, people stray into dangerous cultic endeavors that may hurt them, even as they seek healing. The church can correct this.

Conclusion:

Our vision for the church's healing ministry is predicated on the belief that healing gifts persist in the church, that the people continue to need healing, and that healing will culminate in increased conversion and eventually evangelism. The church needs to reestablish her prominence in healing so

We believe that spirituality without religious training and Christian spiritual fail-safes has allowed people to engage in practices that are harmful to them in body, mind, and spirit.

that the unchurched but spiritually needy public does not fall into occult practices to satisfy spiritually related healing needs. Psychiatry and psychology are not fully equipped to handle the spiritual aspects of mental illness. A church that is competent to heal in Jesus name is a necessary institution to which Christian doctors and psychologists can refer their patients. The church also has a special ministry to alternative medicine, which has become influenced by occult religious ideas. No impediment exists to prevent the church from assuming a more intense healing effort. Scripture, tradition, and reason support the church's authority to continue Our Lord's supernatural ministry to the psyche and soma. In short, it is time to heal.

References

Brennan, B (1987). *Hands of light.* New York: Bantam.

Gerber, R (1988). *Vibrational medicine.* Sante Fe: Bear & Company.

Matthews, D. Larson, D. and Barry, C. (1993). *The faith factor: An annotated bibliography of clinical research on spiritual subjects* (Vol. I & II). National Institute for Healthcare Research.

Ratzinger, J, Imprimi Potest (1995). *Catechism of the catholic church.* New York: Doubleday.

Sheler, J (1997). Heaven in the age of reason. *US News and World Report*, March 31, 65-66.

Woodward, K (1997). Is god listening? *Newsweek*, March 31, 57-65.

Varuschka DeMarici, Psy.D. practices at the University of Pennsylvania. Dr. De-Marici has lectured throughout the world about Christian psychology and the impact of divine grace upon mental suffering. She has a reputation as an excellent lecturer and seminar leader. Her radio show Hope for Healing *was considered a fascinating contribution to integrating the field of psychology with Christian spirituality.*

The Argument for the Inclusion of Spirituality

Charles L. Zeiders, Psy.D.
James L. Schaller, M.D., M.A.R.

Framing the arguments for and against spirituality and religion in mental health theory and practice, this article supplies manifold examples of reviewed scientific evidence to support the notions that spirituality can be empirically distinguished as an expressly positive force in mental health. Such findings support the yearnings of many patients and practitioners to include the spiritual in mental health theory and practice. It is suggested, however, that exuberance for the spiritual—however based in research—should balance itself with an understanding of the existing impediments to the inclusion of spirituality in mainstream clinical and academic psychology and psychiatry, suggesting that even more research will be required before the establishment of widespread acceptance.

A re spiritual people psychologically immature? Does religion help the mind? Arguments for and against spirituality and religion are not new within the mental health disciplines. Until lately, the argument against or indifference to spirituality has been the ascendant one. An accumulation of recent research, however, suggests that religious and spiritually oriented people are benefiting from their faith. Such data supports patients and practitioners of psychology and psychiatry who seek to include the spiritual in their theoretical paradigms and practical intervention. Important impediments exist, however, that prevent spirituality and religion from finding greater acceptance in the fields of mental health—suggesting that still more research will have to be conducted before this aspect of human experience is incorporated into the mental health equations by which psychologists and psychiatrists operate.

Spirituality: Unscientific, Infantile, Pathological

One school of thought advocates that spirituality is unscientific, infantile, and pathological. Freud held all three views. His biographer Gay (1988) interprets

---

* This article was first published in *The Journal of Christian Healing*, Volume 20, #1, Spring, 1998, pp. 33-45.

Encounters with the divine, ... have the capacity to console, heal, and pull individuals to higher levels of health and maturity.

If religion—from the most primitive sacrifice to the most elaborate theology—is infantile fear, awe, and passivity carried over into adult life, then science, as a psychoanalyst might put it, is an organized effort to get beyond childishness. The scientist disdains the pathetic effort of the believer to realize fantasies through pious wanting and ritual performances ... (p. 534)

Agreeing with Freud, emphasizing the pathological, some psychiatrists have labeled spirituality "Borderline psychosis ... A regression, an escape, a projection upon the world of a primitive infantile state" (Group for the Advancement of Psychiatry, 1976). Some reduce spirituality simply to a "psychotic episode" (Horton, 1974) or localize it to a reductionistic "temporal lobe dysfunction" (Mandel, 1980). Ellis associated the religious with the irrational and expected it to lead to poor mental health (Worthington, Kurusu, McCullough, and Sandage, 1996). The National Academy of Sciences (1996) supported Freud's ideology that religion was not compatible with science by their contention that spirituality and science were "mutually exclusive realms of thought."

Spirituality: Verifiable, Mature, and Healthy
Another school of thought seeks to marry spirituality and science, facilitate human maturation through spirituality, and harness health from it. Deikman (1980) argued that spirituality represents "a non-ordinary door to satisfaction." He lamented that

our cultural bias ... tells us that [spiritual] states are unreal, pathological, 'crazy' or 'regressive;' it is a bias that declares the entire area to be 'subjective' and, therefore, 'unscientific.' We have been indoctrinated neither to make use of nor to look closely at these realms ... under the banner of the scientific method our thinking has been constricted. It is time we made the [spiritual] ... a legitimate option for ourselves and for science (p. 268).

Psychologists William James (1902) and Evelyn Underhill (1910) studied spiritual experience of ordinary people and great mystics. Encounters with the divine, they concluded, have the capacity to console, heal, and pull individuals to higher levels of health and maturity. More recently Peck (1978) observed that a supernatural health force or "grace," may operate not only to beat pathology but to nurture and spur individuals into a developmental epoch of "Spiritual Competence."

A new and growing body of empirical evidence supports this latter school of thought. Spirituality can be scientifically studied, and it can be established that spiritual people benefit from their spirituality measurably and in the direction of psychological and physical health.

Religious Commitment and Well-being

Studies show that spirituality has beneficial effects upon important measures of well-being. A cross-sectional survey designed by Ellison and George (1994) concluded that church attendance improves the quantity and quality of social support. Heart surgery patients who identify themselves as "deeply religious" tend to have lower postoperative mortality rates (Oxman, 1995). A survey of adults (Hadaway & Roof, 1978) found that the importance of religion directly related to feeling worthwhile and that worthwhileness was also tied to church attendance. A study of childhood risk factors associated religious involvement with fewer behavior problems and higher maturity measures for children and adolescents (Cohen & Brook, 1987). A survey of college students found that students affiliated with Christian religious groups scored better on indices of well-being than non-affiliated students (Frankel & Hewitt, 1994). McNamara and George (1979) conducted a national survey that found religiosity to be significantly and positively correlated with quality of life measures, including mood, marital satisfaction, family life, and general satisfaction. Glenn & Weaver (1978) also found church attendance to strongly and positively correlate with marital happiness. Patients with hip fractures and high religious commitment experience greater well-being than non-religious patients, as measured by lower depression scores and an ability to walk farther distances at discharge (Pressman, Lyons, Larson, & Strain, 1990). Religiously involved adolescents have lower rates of delinquency, alcohol, and drug use than less spiritual peers (Burkett & White, 1974). In a national survey sample, using a religiously oriented survey instrument, Watson, Hood, Morris and Hall (1985) found that viewing religion as the central end around which life is organized positively relates to self-esteem. Overall, findings seem to suggest that going to church and keeping spirituality as a central life focus predicts, and/or correlates with doing well on various measures of well-being.

Spirituality and Psychopathology

In addition to positively correlating with indices of well-being, spirituality may negatively correlate with psychopathology. Church attendance is inversely related to the development of diagnosable mental disorders (Koenig, George, Meador, Blazer, and Dyck, 1994) and religious practices such as prayer, scriptural study and church attendance decreases the risk of developing alcoholism (Koenig, George, Meador, and Ford, 1994). Religious people tend to have better moods than non-religious people (McNamara & George, 1979). Older persons with intrinsic religiosity are less likely to have anxiety about death than younger persons with less religiosity (Thorson & Powell, 1990). Young people also fear death less if they are religious (Richardson, Berman, Piwowarski, 1983). Religiosity was negatively correlated with deviant attitudes and deviant behavior in a sample of high school and college students (Rohrbaugh & Jessor, 1975). Emotional health of caregivers to chronically ill people positively correlates to religious faith (Rabins, Fitting, Eastham, and Fetting, 1990). Hospitalized elderly men who cope using religion have lower depression scores than less religious peers (Koenig, Cohen, Blazer, Pieper, Meador, Shelp, Goli, and DiPasquale, 1992). Public religiosity is associated with lower depression risks for disabled men (Idler & Kasl, 1992). Religiousness is negatively associated with drug use among teenagers (Hays, Stacy, Widaman, DiMatteo, and Downey, 1986). Religious adults are less likely to have psychiatric symptoms than nonreligious adults (Hannay, 1980). People who attend religious services at least once a month report fewer psychological symptoms than those with no religious affiliation (Hannay, 1980). Religious belief correlates inversely with schizotypal thinking in normal subjects (Feldman & Rust, 1989). A survey of one hundred thirty two 15-year-old girls found that positive attitudes toward religion negatively correlate with psychotic personality traits (Francis & Pearson, 1985). Opioid addicts who participated in a religious treatment program remained abstinent at a one year follow-up, compared to 5% of addicts who underwent a non-religious treatment program (Desmond & Maddux, 1981). Harvard divinity students who have undergone a deep spiritual experience score lower on indices of hostility and higher on measures of self-confidence in the face of stress than peers who have not experienced their "ground of being" (Kass, 1996, SP1). Nine empirical studies have been conducted since 1951 that negatively correlate four dimensions of spiritual wellness (meaning in life, intrinsic values, transcendence, or membership to spiritual community) to depression, showing empirical "support for a relationship between depression and each of the four dimensions of spiritual wellness" (Westgate, 1996, 32).

Prayer and Psychologically Relevant Findings

Just as spirituality and religion can predict low psychological symptomatology, several empirical studies suggest that prayer correlates with psychologically positive findings. Questionnaire research conducted with 100 AA members in southern California found that prayer was positively correlated with life purpose and length of sobriety (Carroll, 1993). Of over 300 randomly selected people suffering from musculoskeletal pain, 44% of respondents reported praying to cope with pain, 54% of that group further report-

Overall, findings seem to suggest that going to church and keeping spirituality as a central life focus predicts doing well on various measures of well-being.

ing, that prayer was "very helpful" (Cronan, Kaplan, Posner, Blumberg, & Kozin, 1989). In a survey of 100 Catholic widows, researchers found 89% declared prayer useful for coping with husband loss (Gass, 1987). Prayer research has also shown frequency of prayer to positively associate with marital adjustment (Gruner, 1985). Use of prayer negatively relates to death anxiety in older adults (Koenig, 1988). For sixth and seventh graders in a longitudinal study, prayer with parents negatively related to alcohol use (Long & Boik, 1993). For 560 randomly sampled adults in Akron, Ohio, frequent prayer positively related to existential well-being (Poloma & Pendleton, 1991). Frequent prayer and spiritual experience during prayer, like feeling energy or feeling God's presence, positively relate to purpose in life (Richards, 1990, 1991). In a survey of 100 coronary surgery patients, 95 reported using prayer as a coping behavior, with 70 rating prayer "very helpful" to help them deal with the ordeal (Saudia, Kinney, Brown, and Young-Ward, 1991). A survey of 25 cancer patients found that, of the spiritual strategies available, prayer was the strategy patients used most frequently to cope (Sondestrom & Martinson, 1987). In a survey of Illinois physicians who pray with older patients, researchers found that 89.3 percent of the physicians felt that praying with older patients helped patients somewhat or a great deal (Koenig, Lucille, Dayringer, 1989). In a double blind experiment comparing prayed-for and not prayed-for coronary patients, Byrd (1988) found that prayed-for patients required fewer antibiotics, had less pulmonary edema, and needed fewer intubations. A survey of cystic fibrosis patients and their families showed that the most common non-medical treatment used by respondents was group prayer, with 93% of frequent group prayer users perceiving benefit from this prayers (Stern, Cana, Doershunk, 1992). A group of college students practicing standardized prayer experienced decrease in muscle tension and scored lower on indices of anger and anxiety than counterparts practicing secular progressive relaxation (Carlson, Bacasta, and Simanton, 1988). Survey data indicate that a strong connection exists between frequent prayer and positive behavior towards others, and in interview situations people who prayed frequently were judged by raters to be more cooperative and friendly (Morgan, 1983). A review of 150 studies of prayer and prayer-like techniques used to produce positive effects on enzymes, plants, animals, and people, found that over half of these scientific studies yielded significant, positive results, leading one reviewer to note that if "healing were a medication it would be on the market" (Benor, 1992, 74).

The Need for Psychiatry and Psychology to Not Exclude the Religious

From the above, one notes that medical and social science has produced a plethora of information contradicting anti-spiritual bias in psychiatry and psychology. Some reviewers have found religion to have a positive impact on clinical results 84 percent of the time. These findings present a strong argument for the inclusion of spirituality in psychiatric and psychological treatment plans. This positive inclusion of spiritual considerations and interventions are demanded by demographic realities: 95% of the American population believes in God, 50% pray daily, and 40% attend religious services (Gallup, Report #236, 1985; Bergin & Jensen, 1990). But not only are many American people spiritual, they want their caregivers to respect their spirituality and address their care needs on that level: 77% of patients feel that physicians should consider their spiritual needs, 48 % of patients want their physician to pray with them, and 37 % of patients want their physician to discuss religious beliefs with them (King & Bushwick 1994). Further survey data suggests that caregivers such as psychologists would be willing to move in that direction: 75% of surveyed psychologists felt that religious issues were within the scope of the clinical setting, and 90% felt that asking about and understanding their clients' religious backgrounds was clinically important (Shaftanske & Malony, 1990). All this points to the current need in psychiatry and psychology for religious and spiritual literacy. Since empirical evidence exists to support the health efficacy of the spiritual, and since both clients and some care givers respect spirituality, and since both clients and some care givers want to share with one another in spiritual terms, there is—in short—a need to do so.

The Ongoing Struggle for Acceptance

Despite promising research and grass-roots support for inclusion of spirituality in mental health, acceptance is likely to be a difficult. Three factors account for this. First, psychology and psychiatry have absorbed and demystified the mental healing mission originally conducted by the church, and those disciplines may not wish to incorporate spirituality from a vanquished way of healing. Second, the current mental health paradigm is a-religious. By nature, paradigms remain impervious to extra-paradigmatic information; so the existing structure may remain impervious or at least highly resistant to extra-paradigmatic spirituality, despite compelling new evidence. Third, a practitioner's own psychological issues and counter-resistance to the demanding aspects of the religious experience, may prevent mental health theoreticians (and policy brokers) from making the divine admissible in the treatment arena. These hurdles warrant further elaboration.

Before the existence of psychology and psychiatry in Western civilization, the Christian church ministered to psychological needs. In the fourth century, for example, John Chrysostom developed treatments for grief, and in the early 16th century, Martin Luther developed instructions for consoling an anxious man (Clebsh and Jackie, 1983). With the rise of theistic science and the tide of antireligious sentiment that eventually came from its children, the mental health mission of the church lost ground to reductonistic psychology and psychiatry. Despite the inclusion of the new "V" code for spiritual and religious problems in the *DSM-IV* (APA, 1994) and the apparent explosion of new religious treatment research, the mental health establishment may remain loath to incorporate spirituality from traditions that appear to have lost their ministry and authority in this area to scientific psychology and psychiatry.

The next hurdle that impedes the inclusion of spirituality into mental health involves the nature of paradigms. In *The Structure of Scientific Revolutions* (1962), Kuhn argues that scientists bring to the table ultimate metaphysical presuppositions, often unconscious, which cause them to dismiss legitimate scientific evidence. Kuhn teaches that the only way an ultimate presuppositional scientific paradigm can be challenged is when vast amounts of data cannot be made to fit into the paradigm. Since theorists are ingenious at explaining away data that contradicts their ultimate presuppositions (e.g. a "square" is really two of my triangles fitting neatly into my triangle paradigm) a vast amount of conclusive research will have to be accomplished before the existing paradigm accepts the revolutionary finding that spirituality benefits mental health.

Finally, psychological and existential factors may influence brokers of mental health theory and practice in such a manner that they disavow the spiritual in their professional work for personal reasons. For example, Vitz (1990) demonstrates that famous thinkers of the past have had one or both of their parents leave them through death, abandonment, or abuse. Votaire, Feuerbach, Neitzsche, and Bertrand Russell are examples of men whose "orphan psychology" (Schaller, 1995) influenced their agnostic or atheistic stance. Someone who experiences a poor relationship with a parent can generalize this experience to an unconsciously motivated yet profound rejection of God; therefore, they reject God, not based on scientific data, but due to their unconscious, unmetabolized woundedness. These dynamics can influence the attitudes of mental health theorists and practitioners against spirituality,

Moreover, religion throughout history has posed an existential threat to humans. If God exists, there may be certain obligations and elements of accountability which may intimidate the beholder of the divine. Indeed, in the Hindu religion, God as Kali is depicted with fangs and skulls hanging around her neck. In Judaic and Christian scripture, God is not merely loving and forgiving but also a holy and fearsome judge. We should appreciate the dynamics of psychologists and psychiatrists who avoid embracing religion and spirituality, because of possible core psychological fears, wounds and object-relations problems, where God is not merely caring but also One to Whom one is accountable. Existential intimidation can lead psychologists and psychiatrists to deny spiritual realities.

Conclusion

Scientific evidence has been mounting to support the notion that religious and spiritual beliefs and practices represent beneficial factors for improving mental health. While existing new research contradicts the anti-spirituality argument, and lends credibility to the yearning of many patients and practitioners to include spirituality within the scope of mental health theory and practice, it will take years to develop a widespread acceptance of the importance of spirituality within psychology and psychiatry. Reasons for this include the assumption and de-mystification of the church's mental health ministry, the nature of scientific paradigms, and finally human nature itself. An overabundance of more evidence will be needed to establish a positive place for spirituality within the realm of mental health.

References*

American Psychiatric Association (1994). *Diagnostic and statistics manual of mental disorders,* 4th edition, Washington, DC: Author.

Benor, D. (1992). Lessons from spiritual healing research and practice. *Subtle Energies, 3,* 73-88.

Benson, H. (1996a). *Welcome and introduction: The genesis of the course.* Paper presented at Spirituality & Healing in Medicine - II, Boston, MA, December, 1996.

Benson, H. (1996b). *Timeless healing: The power and biology of belief.* New York: Scribner.

Bergin, A., & Jensen, J. (1990). Religiosity of psychotherapists: A national survey. *Psychotherapy 27* (1) 3-7.

Burkett, S., & White, M. (1974). Hellfire and delinquency: Another look. *Journal for the Scientific Study of Religion. 13* (D), 455-462.

Byrd, R. (1988). Positive therapeutic effects of therapeutic prayer in a coronary care unit population. *Southern Medical Journal, 81,* 826-829.

Carlson, C., Bacaseta, P., & Simanton, D. (1988). A controlled evaluation of devotional meditation and progressive relaxation. *Journal of Psychology and Theology. 16,* 362-368.

Caroll, S. (1993). Spirituality and purpose in life in alcoholism recovery. *Journal of Studies in Alcohol, 54,* 297-301.

Clebsh, W., & Jaekle, C. (1994). *Pastoral care in historical perspective.* New York: Jason Aronson.

Cohen, P., & Brook, J. (1987). Family factors related to the persistence of psychopathology in childhood and adolescence, *Psychiatry, 50,* 332-345,

Cronan, T., Kaplan, R., Posner, L., Blumberg, E., & Kozin, F. (1989). Prevalence of the use of unconventional remedies for arthritis in a metropolitan community. *Arthritis and Rheumatism, 32,* 1604-1607.

Deikman, A. (1980). Bimodal consciousness and the mystic experience, In R.

Woods (Ed.), *Understanding mysticism: Its meaning, its methodology, interpretation in world religions, psychological evaluations, philosophical and theological appraisals* (pp.261-269). Garden City, NY: Image Books.

Desmond, D., & Maddux, J. (1981). Religious programs in careers of chronic heroin users, *American Journal of Drug and Alcohol Abuse, 8* (1), 71-83.

Ellison, C., & George, L. (1994). Religious involvement, social ties and social support in a southwestern community, *Journal for the Scientific Study of Religion, 33* (1), 46-61.

Feldman, J., & Rust, J. (1989). Religiosity, schizotypal thinking, and schizophrenia. *Psychological Reports, 65,* 587-593.

Francis, L., & Pearson, P. (1985). Psychoticism and religiosity among 15 year olds. *Personality and Individual Differences, 6* (3), 397-398.

Frankel, B., & Hewitt, W. (1994). Religion and well-being among Canadian university students: The role of faith groups on campus. *Journal for the Scientific Study of Religion, 33* (1), 62-73.

Gallup, J (1985). Report #236. *100 Questions and answers: Religion in America.* Princeton, NJ: Princeton Religious Research Center.

Gass, K. (1987). Coping strategies for widows. *Journal of Gerontological Nursing, 13,* 29-33.

Gay, P. (1988), *Freud: A life for our time.* New York: W.W. Norton & Company.

Glenn, N., & Weaver, C. (1978). A multivariate, multisurvey of marital happiness. *Journal of Marriage and the Family, 40* (2), 269-282.

Group for the Advancement of Psychiatry. (1976). *Mysticism: Spiritual quest or mental disorder.* No further citation provided in Larson and Matthews (1996). *Spirituality and medical outcomes.* Paper presented at Spirituality & Healing in Medicine—II, Boston, MA, December, 1996.

Gruner, L. (1985). The correlation of private, religious devotional practices and marital adjustment. *Journal of Comparative Family Studies, 16,* 47-59.

Hadaway, C., & Roof, W. (1978). Religious commitment and the quality of life in American society. *Review of Religious Research, 19* (3), 295-307.

Hannay, D. (1980). Religion and health. *Social Science and Medicine, 14* (A), 683-685.

Hays, R., Stacy, A., Widaman, Dimetteo, M., & Downey, R. (1986). Multistage path models of adolescent alcohol and drug use: A reanalysis. *Journal of Drug Issues, 16* (3). 357-369.

Horton, P. (1974). The mystical experience: Substance of an illusion. *American Psychoanalytic Association Journal, 22* (1-2), 364-380.

Idler, E., & Kasl, S. (1992). Religion, disability, depression and the timing of death. *American Journal of Sociology, 97* (4), 1052-1079.

James, W. (1902). *The varieties of religious experience: A study in human nature.* Cambridge, MA: Harvard University Press, 1985. (Original edition 1902).

Kass, J. (1996). Tapping into something greater than ourselves. *Spirituality & Health, Fall,* SPI-SP7.

King, D., & Bushwick, B. (1994). Beliefs and attitudes of hospital inpatients about faith healing and prayer. *Journal of Family Practice, 39* (4), 349-352.

Koenig, H., George, L., Meador, K., Blazer, D., & Dyck, P, (1994). Religious affiliation and psychiatric disorder among Protestant baby boomers. *Hospital and Community Psychiatry, 45* (6),586-596.

Koenig, H., George, L., Meador, K., & Ford, S. (1994). Religious practices and alcoholism in a southern adult population. *Hospital and Community Psychiatry, 45* (3), 225-231.

Koenig, H., Cohen, M., Blazer, D., Pieper, C., Meador, K., Shelp, S., Goli, V., & DiPasquale, B. (1992). Religious coping and depression among elderly hospitalized medically ill men. *American Journal of Psychiatry, 149* (12), 1693-1700.

Koenig, H. (1988). Religious behaviors and death anxiety in later life. *The Hospice Journal 4*, 3-24.

Koenig, H., Lucille, B., & Dayringer, R. (1989). Physician perspectives on the role of religion in the physician—older patient relationship. *The Journal of Family Practice, 28*, 441-448.

Kuhn, T. (1962). *The structure of scientific revolutions.* Chicago: University of Chicago Press.

Long, D., & Biok, R. (1993). Predicting alcohol abuse in rural children: A longitudinal study. *Nursing Research, 42*, 79-86.

Mandel, A. (1980). In R.J. Davidson (Ed.), *The psychology of consciousness.* No further citation provided in Larson and Matthews (1996). *Spirituality and medical outcomes.* Paper presented at Spirituality & Healing in Medicine—II, Boston, MA, December, 1996.

McNamara, P., & George, A. (1979). Measures of religiosity and the quality of life. In D.O. Moberg (Ed.), *Spiritual Well-being: Sociological Perspectives* (pp. 229-236). Washington, D.C.: University Press of America.

Morgan, S. (1983). A research note on religion and morality: Are religious people nice people? *Social Forces, 61*, 683-692.

National Academy of Sciences. *Science and creationism: A view from the national academy of sciences.* No further citation provided in Larson and Matthews (1996). *Spirituality and Medical Outcomes.* Paper presented at Spirituality & Healing in Medicine - II, Boston, MA, December, 1996.

Oxman, T, (1995). The lack of social participation or religious strength and comfort as risk factors for death after cardiac surgery in the elderly. *Psychosomatic Medicine, 57*, 5-15.

Poloma, M., & Pendleton, B. (1991). The effects of prayer and prayer experiences on measures of general well-being. *Journal of Psychology and Theology, 19*, 71-83.

Peck, M. (1978). *The road less traveled.* New York: Simon & Schuster.

Pressman, P., Lyons, J., Larson, S., & Strain, J. (1990). Religious belief, depression, and ambulation status in elderly women with broken hips. *American Journal of Psychiatry, 147*,758-760.

Rabins, P., Fitting, M., Eastham, J. & Fetting, J. (1990). The emotional impact of caring for the chronically ill. *Psychosomatics, 31* (3), 331-336.

Richards, D. (1990). A "universal forces" dimension of locus of control in a population of spiritual seekers. *Psychological Reports, 67*, 847-850.

Richards, D. (1991). The phenomenology and psychological correlates of verbal prayer. *Journal of Psychology and Theology, 19*, 354-363.

Richardson, V., Berman, S., & Piwowarski, M. (1983). Projective assessment of the relationship between the salience of death, religion and age among adults in America. *Journal of General Psychology, 109*, 149-156.

Rohrbaugh, J. & Jessor, R. (1975). Religiosity in youth: A personal control against deviant behavior. *Journal of Personality, 43* (1), 136-155.

Saudia, T., Kinney, M., Brown, K., & Young-Ward, L. (1991). Health locus of control and helpfulness of prayer. *Heart and Lung, 20*, 60-65.

Schaller, J. (1995). *The search for lost fathering.* Grand Rapids, MI: Fleming Revell.

Shafranske, E., & Malony, H. (1990). Clinical psychologists' religious and spiritual orientation and their practice of psychology. Meeting of the American Psychological Association. *Psychotherapy, 27* (1), 72-78.

Sondestrom, K., & Martinson, I. (1997). Patients' spiritual coping strategies: A study of nurse and patient perspectives. *Oncology Nursing Forum, 14*, 41-46.

Stern, R., Cana, E., & Doershuk, C. (1992). Use of nonmedical treatment by cystic fibrosis patients. *Journal of Adolescent Health, 13*, 612-615.

Thorson, J., & Powell, F. (1990). Meanings of death and intrinsic religiosity. *Journal of Clinical Psychology, 46* (4), 379-391.

Underhill, E. (1910). *Mysticism: The preeminent study in the nature and development of spiritual consciousness.* New York: Doubleday. (Original edition 1910).

Vitz, P. (1990). The psychology of atheism and Christian spirituality. *Anthropes, 6*, 99.

Watson, P., Hood, R., Morris, R., & Hall, J. (1985). Religiosity sin, and self-esteem. *Journal of Psychology and Theology, 13* (2), 116-128.

Westgate, C. (1996). Spiritual wellness and depression. *Journal of Counseling and Development, 75* (1), 26-35.

Worthington, E., Kurusu, T., McCullough, M. & Sandage, S.(1996). Empirical research on religion and psychotherapeutic processes and outcomes: A 10-year, review and research prospectus. *Psychological Bulletin. 119* (3), 448-487.

James Schaller, M.D., M.A.R. is a doctor, an adult psychiatrist, a fellow in child and adolescent psychiatry, frequent mental health radio show guest, and a theologian. He was associated with the Eastern Pennsylvania Psychiatric Institute and is now in private practice in Naples, FL, working both clinically and as a researcher, in addition to being a graduate level counseling and psychology teacher. He is author of The Search for Lost Fathering, *along with a number of other academic psychiatry articles. He is one of only a few theologically trained child and adult psychiatrists in the country.*